RaNae Merrill

Sideways Spiral QUILTS

Design and Sew Chains, Ropes and Ribbons

Quilt by Betsy Vinegrad, see page 2 for description

RaNae Merrill Quilt Design
New York, New York

www.ranaemerrillquilts.com

Sideways Spiral Quilts: Design and Sew Chains, Ropes and Ribbons
Copyright © 2016 by RaNae Merrill.

PUBLISHED BY
RaNae Merrill Quilt Design
370 West 118th Street #2D
New York, NY 10026
212-316-2063
www.ranaemerrillquilts.com
info@ranaemerrillquilts.com

COVER/BOOK DESIGN: Page + Pixel
PHOTOGRAPHY: RaNae Merrill and Rory Polo, except
Page 18: Photos courtesy of Alvin & Company, Inc.
Pages 56 & 71: Nienke Smit

ISBN: 978-1-942853-03-9

11 12 13 14 15   5 4 3 2 1

Available at:
www.CreateSpace.com/6177408
www.amazon.com
www.ranaemerrillquilts.com

ON THE TITLE PAGE:

SPARE CHANGE
Designed, pieced and quilted
by Betsy Vinegrad
53" x 63"

Betsy combined spiral chains with an old Amish pattern
called Chinese Coins. The carefully planned color gradations and the tonal grey background give it a decidedly
modern feel. See a detail of the back on page 162.

About the Author

RaNae Merrill found her calling as a
professional quilter after previous careers
as a pianist, a photographer and a travel
writer. These days she satisfies her
wanderlust by traveling to quilt shows and
guilds as a teacher and lecturer. She has
designed fabrics for Blank Quilting and
has published patterns in a variety of quilt
magazines. When she's not quilting and
writing, you can find her outdoors hiking,
kayaking and skiing. She is a confessed
Spiromaniac: her two previous books
are *Simply Amazing Spiral Quilts* and
Magnificent Spiral Mandala Quilts.

METRIC CONVERSION CHART

CONVERT	TO	MULTIPLY BY
Inches	Centimeters	2.54
Centimeters	Inches	0.4
Feet	Centimeters	30.5
Centimeters	Feet	0.03
Yards	Meters	0.9
Meters	Yards	1.1

Introduction

Even before I started writing books about quilting, I often used spirals as a basic design for my quilts. I always wondered why I was such a "spiromaniac" until one day when I was cleaning out my mother's garage. Among the boxes that she insisted I take home with me was one in which she had saved a few things that were significant to me from each school year. Topping the layers, in its original red box, was my favorite toy when I was in 4th grade: a Spirograph set. That was also the year I learned to sew.

In my first two books, *Simply Amazing Spiral Quilts* and *Magnificent Spiral Mandala Quilts* I looked at spirals from the top down, with the arms of the spirals spinning in classic "galaxy" form. Then one day it occurred to me that we often look at spirals from the side as well—ropes, licorice twists and DNA are all spirals seen from the side. And so I embarked on a new dimension of my spiromania: sideways spirals.

In my exploration of sideways spirals I came up with several forms, including chains, ropes and ribbons. These shapes have appeared in quilt designs for almost as long as quilts have been made, but there wasn't a simple, systematic method of creating them. And so I have written this book to give quilters a simple way to draw and sew these "sideways spirals."

I hope you will use and enjoy it!

HOW TO USE THIS BOOK

The goal of this book is to teach you how to use chains, ropes and ribbons in your own quilt designs. So, Chapters 1, 2 and 3 are set up as a workbook to teach you to draw chains, ropes and ribbons. Each chapter begins with a gallery of original quilts designed and made by my friends and students. I hope these beautiful quilts will inspire you.

Since this is a workbook, you might find it useful to have it spiral-bound so it will lay flat.

Chains, ropes and ribbons can all be drawn easily within a simple track. The process of setting up the track and drawing the design is shown step-by-step in a series of simple diagrams within each chapter. Using a plastic page protector and dry-erase marker, trace each diagram to learn the process. Once you are familiar with that form, it is a simple matter to adapt it to your own quilt design.

Chapter 4 will teach you how to turn your chain, rope or ribbon design into a quilt, with creative ideas, guidance on fabric choices, and assembly instructions.

Finally, Chapter 5 contains six easy projects - two using spiral chains, two using ropes and two using ribbons. Each project can be easily adapted to different sizes and shapes to fit your imagination.

ONLINE RESOURCES

The Sideways Spirals Blog
https://sidewaysspirals.wordpress.com
Password: Si2de0waLys6
The online library is on this blog. In the course of writing, I had the pleasure of working with a group of very talented and adventurous quilters who helped to test my instructions and ideas as they made sample quilts for the book. The Sideways Spirals Blog is where we all communicated and shared the process, and it is now the online supplement to the book.

For current news, please visit my main blog at *https://ranaemerrillquilts.wordpress.com*.

My website, which hosts my online store, workshop information and other resources, can be found at *www.ranaemerrillquilts.com*.

More information can be found on the Resources page at the end of this book.

Happy quilting!

RaNae

TABLE OF *Contents*

WELCOME BANNER
Designed, sewn and quilted
by Betsy DeVries
7" x 23"

Acknowledgments

My deepest thanks to the wonderful quilters who saw me through the process of drafting, revising and refining my teaching techniques, and in the process designed and made most of the quilts in this book. I could not have done this without you.

Ann White | Lecanto, FL

Barb Adams | Fraser, CO

Barbara Mahaffy | Ancaster, Ontario, Canada

Barbara Shirley | Queensbury, NY

Betsy DeVries | Fraser, CO

Betsy Vinegrad | Short Hills, NJ

Carol Deutcher | Greeley, CO

Cathy Barrow | Mims, FL

Claire Beebe | Olathe, KS

Connie Emmen | Boise, ID

Darlene Folk | Northwood, OH

Deborah Hewitt | Doha, Qatar

Debra Reinert | Philadelphia, PA

Devi Lanphere | Mountain View, CA

Fran Visicaro | Mr. Bethel, PA

Jacquelyn Simpson | Middletown, DE

Jane Hellwege | Bonaire, GA

Joan Shaw | Fraser, CO

Julie Perkins | Adrian, MI

Karen Hostetler | Sunbury, OH

Kathy Radl | Crystal Beach, FL

Leslie Arbuckle | Taylorsville, UT

Leslie Carmichael | Prattville, AL

Linda Ward | Crossfield, Alberta, Canada

Linda Roy | Knoxville, TN

Linda Cooper | Burke , VA

Linda Upp | Sharonville, OH

Marge Reikofski | Norfolk, NE

Mary Dufur | St. John, Virgin Islands

Mary Schwartz | St. Paul, MN

Maureen Czerneda | Dundas, Ontario, Canada

Mavis Abbey | Adelaide, South Australia, Australia

Mel Beach | San Jose, CA

Michael Gustafson | Portland, OR

Miriam Land | Knoxville, TN

Mona Beck | El Cajon, CA

Nancy Proctor | Bayfield, Ontario, Canada

Nienke Smit | Harderwijk, The Netherlands

Noreen Borys | Kingwood, TX

Priscilla Roehm | Jacksonville, FL

Robin Armstead | Copperas Cove, TX

Robin Grube | Redlands, CA

Ruth Shadar | Hod Ha Sharon, Israel

Sherrie Jewson | Kempton, Tasmania, Australia

Susan Arnold | Sunnyvale, CA

Susan Ott | Bradenton, FL

Valerie Harrison | Vankleek Hill, Quebec, Canada

Valerie LeBrun | Greeley, CO

Wanda Barrett | Fraser, CO

Thanks also the other quilters who for various reasons were unable to make quilts, but whose questions and feedback were invaluable in helping me write coherent instructions. And to Rory, who stayed one step ahead of me and brought me Levain Bakery cookies whenever needed.

GRATITUDE
Designed, sewn and quilted by Wanda Barrett
47½˝ x 16½˝

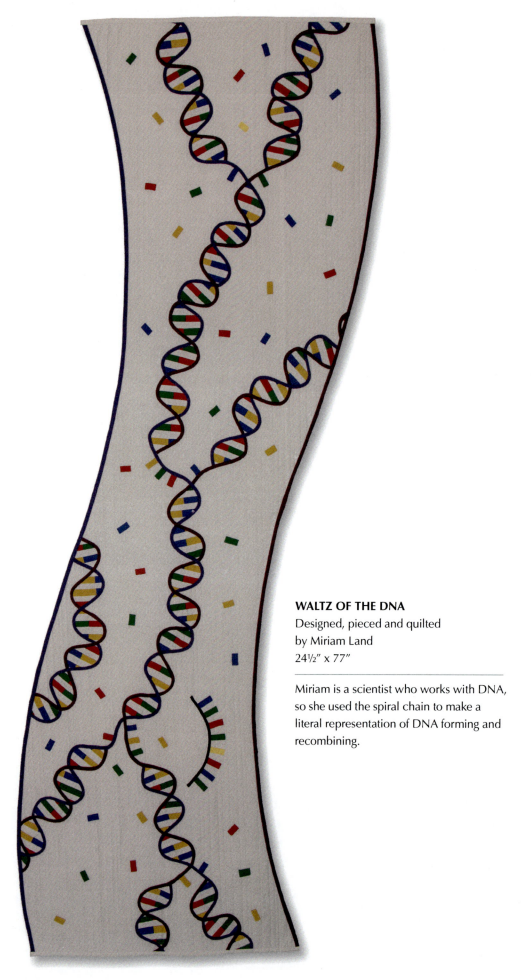

WALTZ OF THE DNA
Designed, pieced and quilted
by Miriam Land
24½" x 77"

Miriam is a scientist who works with DNA,
so she used the spiral chain to make a
literal representation of DNA forming and
recombining.

CHAPTER 1

Spiral Chains

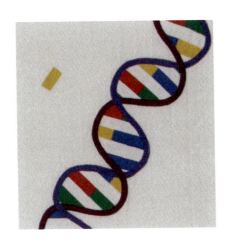

A spiral chain is at the heart of all life on Earth: the DNA molecule. DNA is a double helix spiral that determines every physical attribute of every living thing. It's surprising, then, that something so complex is actually quite easy to draw—seen from the side it's just a couple of intertwined lines.

In a quilt, you can easily create a spiral chain using two lines of bias tape or decorative trim. The spaces created between the bias tape lines are shapes that I call "charms" because the spiral chain reminds me of a charm bracelet. You can fill the charms with anything you want—fussy-cut motifs from a fabric, stenciled letters to spell a name or a phrase, or photographs printed on fabric, for just a few examples.

Creating a quilt with spiral chains is fast and simple—the charms are fused onto the background fabric, then the bias tape is applied around the edges to make the chain.

The next few pages show a gallery of spiral chain quilts, then I'll go on to teach you several easy ways to draw a spiral chain. Choose the method that suits you and give it a spin!

Gallery
of Spiral Chain Quilts

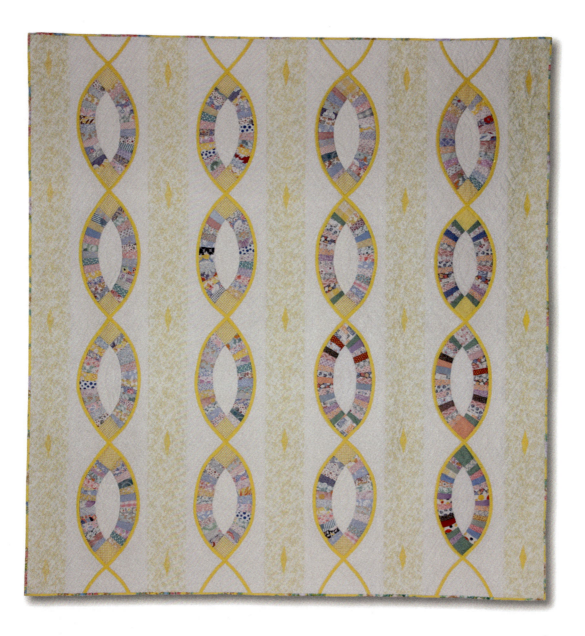

A THOUSAND FIBERS CONNECT US
Designed and pieced by Victoria Findlay-Wolfe
Quilted by Mandy Leins
75" x 77"

Victoria has become known in the quilting world for her modern variations on the traditional double wedding ring design. Here, 1930's vintage hand-pieced "melons" that were intended for a double wedding ring quilt became the charms. Yellow bias tape around the edges makes the spiral chain. (Compare this quilt to Betsy Vinegrad's quilt on the title page.)

WINDBLOWN
Designed, machine pieced, appliquéd,
hand quilted and hand embroidered
by Linda Roy
42" x 42"

I first saw this quilt at Quilt Market in May 2016, and recognized the spiral chain. Linda made it for a guild challenge, "Black & White with a Splash of One Color." It won 3rd Place in the Merit Quilting category of the 2015 *Quilts: A World of Beauty* competition, the annual Judged Show of the International Quilt Association.

MOON FLOWER
Designed, sewn and quilted
by Robin Armstead
69" x 64"

Robin's quilt combines chains, ropes and ribbons, plus loop-de-loops and spirals. The grey hand-dyed fabrics suggesting night and moonlight are not what you might expect as a background for the bright colors of the spirals. Robin always surprises me with her unique vision and color sense!

SIDEWAYS SINE WAVE SPIRALS
Designed, pieced and quilted
by Mel Beach
37½" x 36"

Mel based her design on the mathematical sine wave, which she plotted in Microsoft Excel. By using three lines instead of just two in the spiral chain, she created overlapping spiral chains to create this repeating pattern. She chose colors for the filled areas to suggest transparent overlays.

CHARMED BY FIBONACCI

Designed, pieced and quilted
by Robin Grube
24" x 18"

This spiral chain is shaped into
another spiral based on the
Fibonacci sequence—the same
spiral found in a nautilus shell.

WITH A TWIST OF LIME

Designed, pieced and quilted
by Robin Grube
36" x 36"

A variety of braids and trims stand
in for bias tape giving this simple
spiral chain design an abundance
of texture and whimsy.

SEW LITTLE TIME
Designed, pieced and quilted
by Leslie Carmichael
23" x 53"

A sampler of traditional blocks in
neutral colors forms the background
for this spiral chain with a message
that most quilters can relate to.

HEXIES
Designed, pieced and quilted
by Fran Visicaro
33" x 90"

Fran lives in Pennsylvania, so she and took her
inspiration from Amish hex signs for a design with
a traditional feel. Spiral chains form the yellow
rings in each block, outlined with bias tape the
same yellow as the interior of the charm.

TRICK OR TREAT
Designed, pieced and quilted
by Leslie Carmichael
45" x 40"

The charms of the chain spell
out a holiday message as they
form a path for trick or treaters.
The purple and green bias tapes
are a striking contrast to the
traditional orange and black
colors of Halloween.

WE ARE ALL CONNECTED
Designed, sewn and quilted
by Noreen Borys
28" x 28"

Noreen created spiral chains with
freeform charms, cutting shapes
out of each one to make it unique.
Rather than outline them with bias
tape, she appliquéd each with
machine satin stitch. About this
quilt, Noreen says: "The different
colors represent the different
families and friends we belong to.
The different shapes in each link
represent the different skills and
abilities each one of us has. The
background quilting represents the
connections to others that we may
not even be aware of."

STARS AND SPIRALS
Designed, pieced and quilted
by Connie Emmen
63" x 78½"

Connie embroidered the introductory words of the Declaration of Independence into the charms of this patriotic quilt. She also incorporated different spiral blocks from *Simply Amazing Spiral Quilts*.

Making a Spiral Chain with a Charm Template

If you want uniform size and shape in a spiral chain, begin with the charm. The simplest charm is a pointed oval, but you can get creative and use any shape, as long as the bias tape or trim will go around it. Draft the charms in the size you want, then line them up to create the chain.

WHAT YOU'LL NEED

• Several copies of the page at right

• A pair of scissors

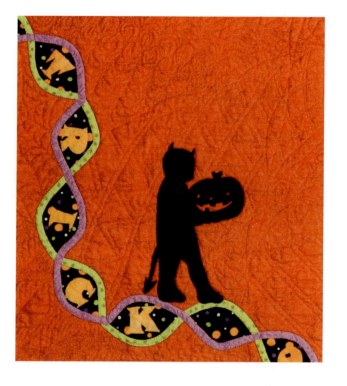

TO MAKE A CHARM CHAIN

Cut out the copied charms. (Use both the "A" and "B" charms - they are the same size.) Arrange the charms with the points touching so that they create a chain. When you make your quilt you'll put bias tape or trim around the edges of the charms to create the chain. Number the charms to keep them in order, if necessary.

Sometimes the outlines of the charms do not flow smoothly as they connect from one charm to the next. Usually the bias tape that forms the chain will smooth out the curve. But if the angle is too tight, it's okay to adjust the shape of the charm a bit to create a better flow.

MAKE A CHARM WINDOW

Print a copy of the charm and cut it out to make a window. Place the window over whatever you want to see in your charm to test the fit, then trace around the window on the fabric to mark the outline of the charm.

TO DRAW YOUR OWN CHARM

Start with a rectangle of paper of the height and width you want your charm to be. Fold it vertically and horizontally to mark the center point of each side. Draw a curve from the midpoint of the long side to the midpoint of the short side. Re-fold the rectangle along the same fold lines and trace the curve, pressing hard enough to mark the other three layers of paper. Re-open and trace the pressure line to complete the charm.

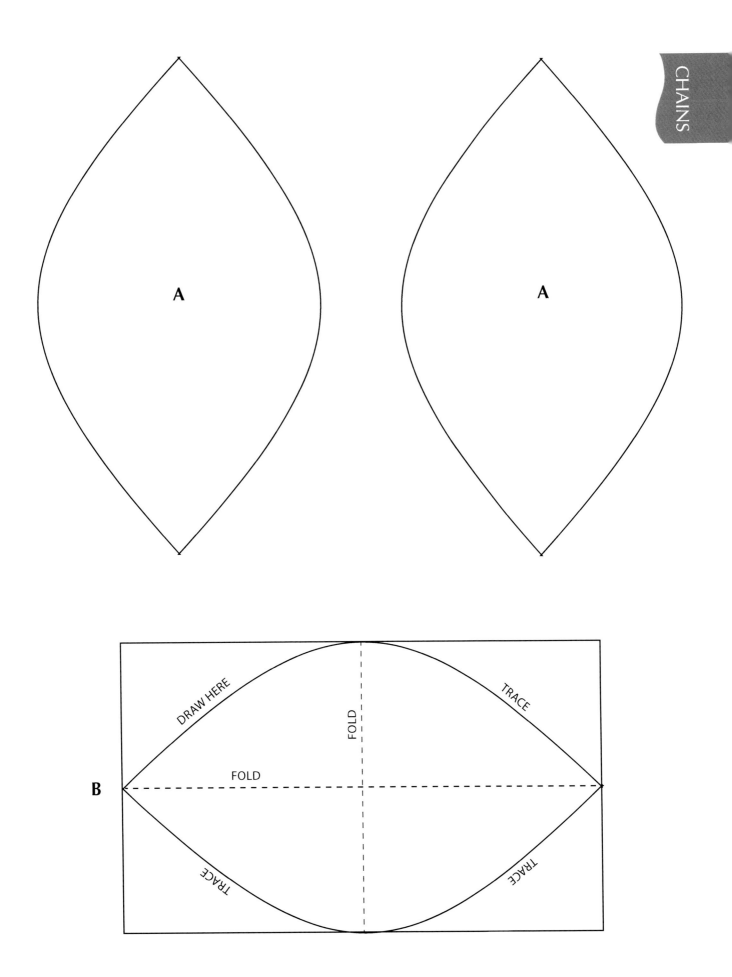

A

A

B

DRAW HERE

TRACE

FOLD

FOLD

FOLD

TRACE

TRACE

Making a Spiral Chain with a Charm Template   **17**

Drawing a Freeform Spiral Chain

Use this technique to create a fun, whimsical chain with charms of random shapes and sizes.

WHAT YOU'LL NEED

- A tracing sheet (clear plastic page protector or tracing paper)
- A dry-erase marker (for a page protector) or a pencil (for tracing paper)
- For erasing: A tissue (for dry-erase markers) or an eraser (for pencil)
- Optional: A flexible curve ruler or French curve template

STEPS

Lay the tracing sheet over the page at right.

1. Trace the blue wavy line.

2. Trace the red wavy line.

Together the two wavy lines create a "DNA" chain. Notice that the lines wave in opposite directions: where the blue line goes right the red line goes left.

TO DRAW YOUR OWN FREEFORM SPIRAL CHAIN

When you draw your own chain, use a sheet of paper the size of your quilt and draw the design freehand at full size. Number the charms to keep them in order when you assemble the quilt. Also mark which end of each charm connects to the next charm (dots in the diagram) to keep them in the correct orientation.

Curves

If you would like more control over the shape of the curves, use a flexible curve ruler or a French curve template. A flexible curve ruler can bend to any shape and hold it.

French curve templates come in many shapes and sizes. I like this one because the interior shapes could be used to draft quilted feathers.

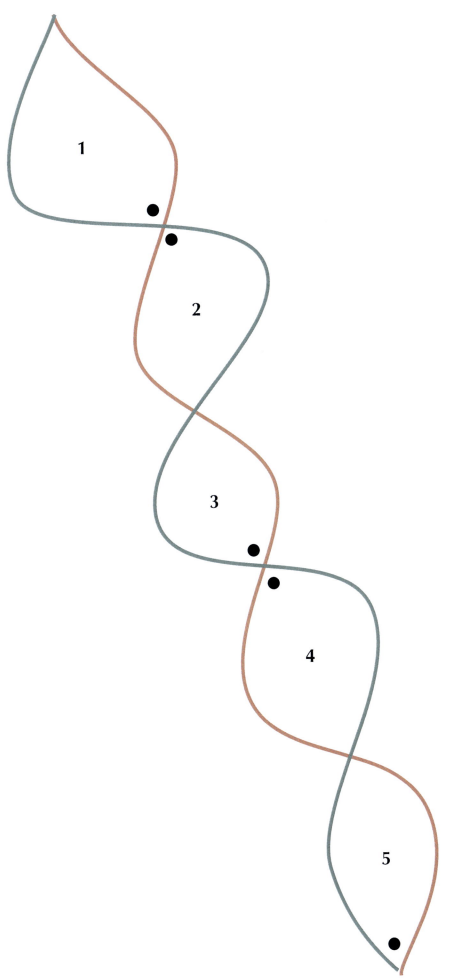

Drawing a Freeform Spiral Chain   **19**

Drawing a Spiral Chain in a Track

Adding a track to the freeform approach on the previous page will give you the ability to control the size and placement of the chain, but keep some variety in the charms. First draw the track and plot the positions of the charms, then draw in the curves.

WHAT YOU'LL NEED

- A tracing sheet (clear plastic page protector or tracing paper)
- A dry-erase marker (for a page protector) or a pencil (for tracing paper)
- For erasing: A tissue (for dry-erase markers) or an eraser (for pencil)
- Optional: A flexible curve ruler or French curve template

STEPS

Lay the tracing sheet over the page at right.

1. Trace the black lines to set up the track.

2. Decide where you want the charms to touch the sides of the track and place dots at these points. Here, trace the black dots.

3. Trace the blue wavy line to draw the first half of the chain. It touches every other dot on alternating sides of the track.

4. Trace the red wavy line to draw the second half of the chain. It touches the remaining open dots on each side of the track.

Together the two wavy lines create the spiral chain. Notice that the lines wave in opposite directions: where the blue line goes right the red line goes left.

TO DRAW YOUR OWN SPIRAL CHAIN IN A TRACK

Use a sheet of paper the size of your quilt and draw the design at full size. You can draw freehand or, if you want more control over the shape of your curves, use a flexible curve ruler or a French curve template to guide the curves. Number the charms to keep them in order when you assemble the quilt. Also mark which end of each charm connects to the next charm (small triangles in the diagram) to keep them in the correct orientation.

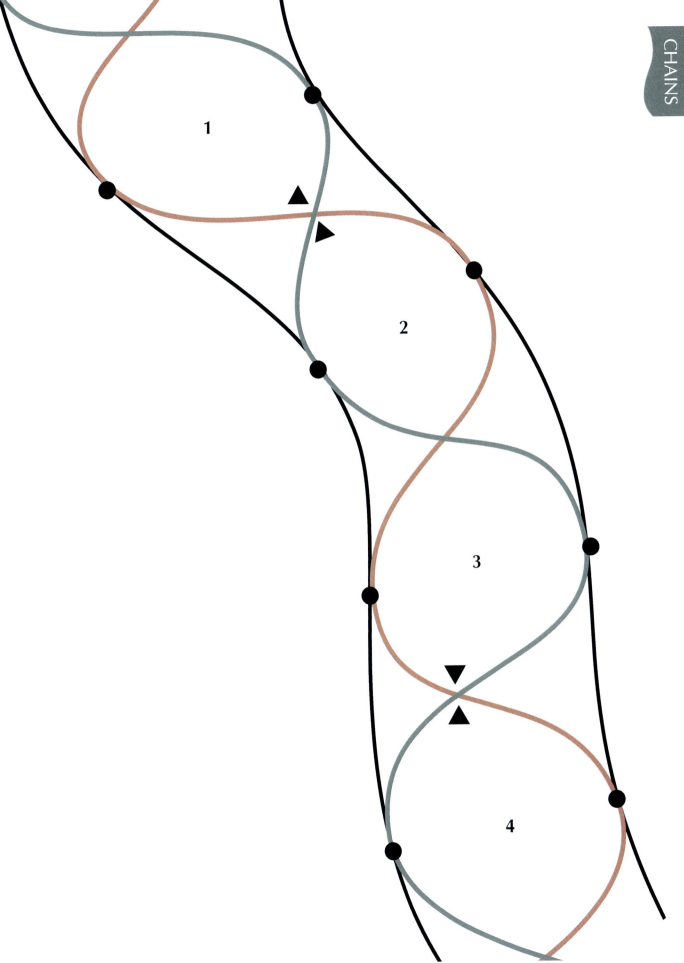

Drawing a Spiral Chain Ring

Drawing a spiral chain ring is easy—just set up the track in the shape of a circle.

WHAT YOU'LL NEED

- A ruler large enough to reach across your circle
- A tracing sheet (plastic page protector or tracing paper)
- A dry-erase marker (for a page protector) or a pencil (for tracing paper)
- For erasing: A tissue (for dry-erase markers) or an eraser (for pencil)

Optional for this exercise, but necessary for drawing your own:

- A drawing compass (for making circles) and a protractor (for measuring angles)

STEPS

Lay the tracing sheet over the page at right and trace the diagram here as you follow the steps below. When you draw your own, follow the same steps on paper.

1. Draw the Outer Circle (A).

2. Draw the Inner Circle (B). (All circles use the same center point.) The distance between the inner circle and the outer circle will be the height of the charm.

3. Draw the Between Circle (C). Notice that this lies about ⅓ of the distance inward from the outer circle.

4. Draw the Vertical Axis (D) all the way across the circles, passing through the center point.

5. Draw the Horizontal Axis across the circles (E), perpendicular to the vertical axis and passing through the center point.

6. Draw diagonal lines (F and G) at a 45 degree angle to (D) and (E) and passing through the center point.

7. Continue drawing other lines across the circles, always passing through the center point (H, I, J, K). Stop drawing lines when the spaces between them are half the width you want the charms to be. You must have an even number of divisions, so always draw the lines completely across the circle, not just from the center to the edge.

8. Draw the charm, using the circles and lines as guides.

9. To draw the rest of the charms, turn the tracing sheet and trace the charm into the remaining spaces around the ring.

NOTE: When drawing your own ring at full size, you may have to experiment and adjust a bit to get the right distance between the circles for the correct size and shape of charm.

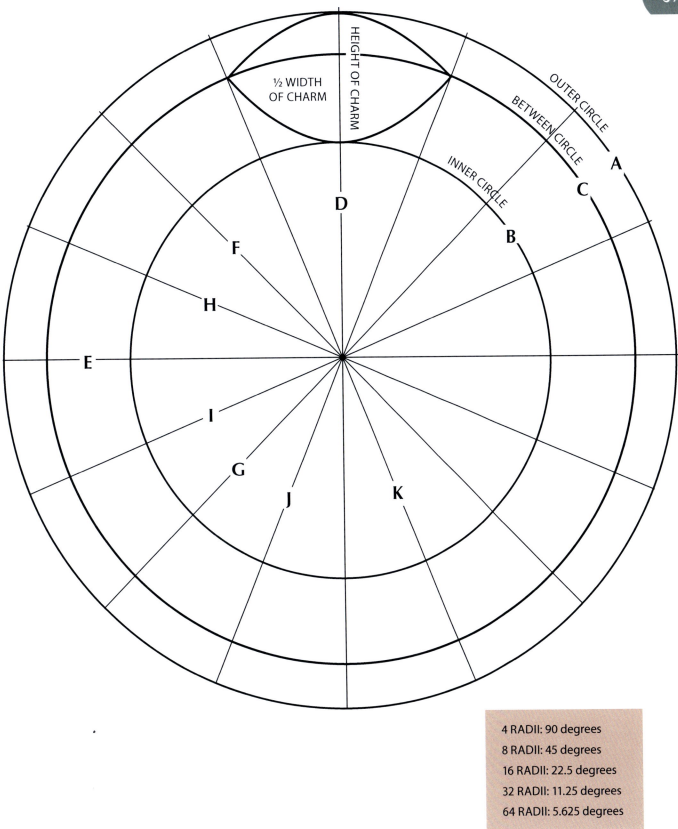

½ WIDTH OF CHARM

HEIGHT OF CHARM

OUTER CIRCLE

BETWEEN CIRCLE

INNER CIRCLE

A

C

B

D

F

H

E

I

G

J

K

4 RADII: 90 degrees
8 RADII: 45 degrees
16 RADII: 22.5 degrees
32 RADII: 11.25 degrees
64 RADII: 5.625 degrees

COLORADO ROCKIES
Designed and pieced by Carol Deutcher
Quilted by Anna Marie Giese
56˝ x 66˝

Carol created a spiral rope frame for her tribute to the Rocky Mountains, her home.

CHAPTER 2

Ropes

A twisted rope is a spiral. When is the last time you used one? If you sewed anything today, the thread you used was a rope—a little, tiny, spiral rope.

Ropes in quilts can make beautiful frames, borders and sashing. They can also be the main focus of the design.

The key to drafting an elegant rope is getting the proportions right. In this section you'll learn a simple technique to draw ropes of any size or shape—straight, curved or circular—by first drawing a track. The track sets up the proportions and acts as a framework for drawing the curves of the twists.

The next few pages contain a gallery of quilts that use ropes as the basis for their designs. Following that are several exercises that you can trace step-by-step to learn to set up a track and draw a rope in it.

When you are ready to draft a rope for your quilt design, set up a track and draw your own rope in the size and shape that suit your design.

Gallery of Rope Quilts

FOREVER WILD
Designed, sewn and quilted
by Leslie Carmichael
41˝ x 41˝

The rope frame couldn't be more
perfect for giving a Western feel
to this charming little quilt.

MIGHTY MOLLUSC
Designed, sewn and quilted
by Deborah Hewitt
46˝ x 32½˝

Of all the quilts made for
this book, I think this one
surprised me the most. I just
never could have imagined
this snail tied up in knots!

SPIRAL REEF
Designed, sewn and quilted
by Connie Emmen
40″ x 30½″

A spiral rope "anchors" this
scene, which also contains
spiral ropes, coiled ribbons and
a Baravelle spiral snail from
Simply Amazing Spiral Quilts.

SPIRAL FISH
Designed, sewn and quilted by Linda Cooper
38″ x 20½″

Ropes form the blue and purple water plants and the body of the eel, while the green
and pink plants are spiral chains. Linda painted the background, fabric and rickrack
with Seta Color, and the fish with airbrush ink. To make the spiral plants she basted the
pieces on Solvy, sewed on the rickrack, dissolved away the Solvy and appliquéd those
pieces on the quilt. The fish are real species embellished by hand-sewing and machine
couching tiny spiral chains for the scales.

STARSHINE CORRALLED
Designed, sewn and quilted by
Marge Reikofski
19″ x 20″

Marge began with a vintage block,
then added the rope borders, sewn
English paper-piecing style and
appliquéd to the white background.
Cathedral window blocks bring the
"starshine" to the corners.

CONFLUENCE
Designed, sewn and quilted
by Susan Arnold
21″ x 21″

Short tapered ropes join in the
center of a circle to create a
unique cross design. A spiral
chain with no charms
forms the circle.

CHARCOIL
Designed, sewn and quilted
by Susan Ott
40˝ x 40˝

Dozens of small rope sections
carefully outlined with narrow
bias tape form a rope that is
only a little bigger than life-size.
Our eyes focus on the elegant
form of the knot because of the
absence of color.

THE REEF KNOT
Designed and sewn
by Valerie Harrison
Quilted by
Colleen Paul
51˝ x 35˝

You can't take the
notion of a rope quilt
more literally than to
design a knot on it!

JUST CHARMING
Designed, sewn, embroidered and quilted
by Ruth Shadar
33″ x 34″

Ruth lives in Israel, can you tell? She is a wonderful quiltmaker and has lately developed a passion for machine embroidery. In this piece she used all the different types of sideways spirals. A rope circle surrounds the center design, then more ropes frame the next diamond and square. Spiral chains make the next border and coiled ribbons finish off the outer edges. Even the quilting is in the form of ropes. What looks like patterned fabric is actually embroidered, and all the pieces are outlined with satin stitch.

UNTITLED

Designed and sewn by Valerie LeBrun
Quilted by Anna Marie Giese
Quilt: 90˝ x 90˝
Wall hanging: 29½˝ x 20½˝

Valerie took a simple, straightforward approach to using ropes in this earthy bed quilt. Warm gradations from violet to brown in the large ropes contrast with the outlines of smaller ropes over a lavender stripe. When she was finished, Valerie used leftover rope sections to make the flower wallhanging at right.

Drawing a Straight Rope

To draw a rope, begin with a track to setup the proportions, then use it as a guide for drawing the curves.

WHAT YOU'LL NEED

- A tracing sheet (clear plastic page protector or tracing paper)

- A dry-erase marker (for a page protector) or a pencil (for tracing paper)

- For erasing: A tissue (for page protector) or an eraser (for tracing paper)

- A clear ruler with a grid (like a rotary-cutting ruler) or a T-square

- Optional: A flexible curve ruler or French curve template (shown on page 18)

STEPS

Lay the tracing sheet over the page at right.

Setting up the track

1. Trace the Center Line. This is where the center of the rope will be.

2. Trace the two Outer Lines—they are parallel to the center line on each side. These are the outside edges of the rope. The lines should be the same distance from the center line. In the example here, the outer lines are 2″ away from the center line, so the completed rope will be 4″ wide. You can make a rope any width you wish.

3. Measure between the outer lines and divide the distance by 8. (In the example shown, 4″ divided by 8 = ½″.) This is the Side Channel Width.

4. Trace the Inner Lines. To find their placement, measure the side channel width inward from the outer lines and draw them parallel to the outer lines. In the example here, the inner lines are ½″ inside the outer lines. The outer lines and the inner lines create the side channel.

Move the tracing sheet to the next page ➡

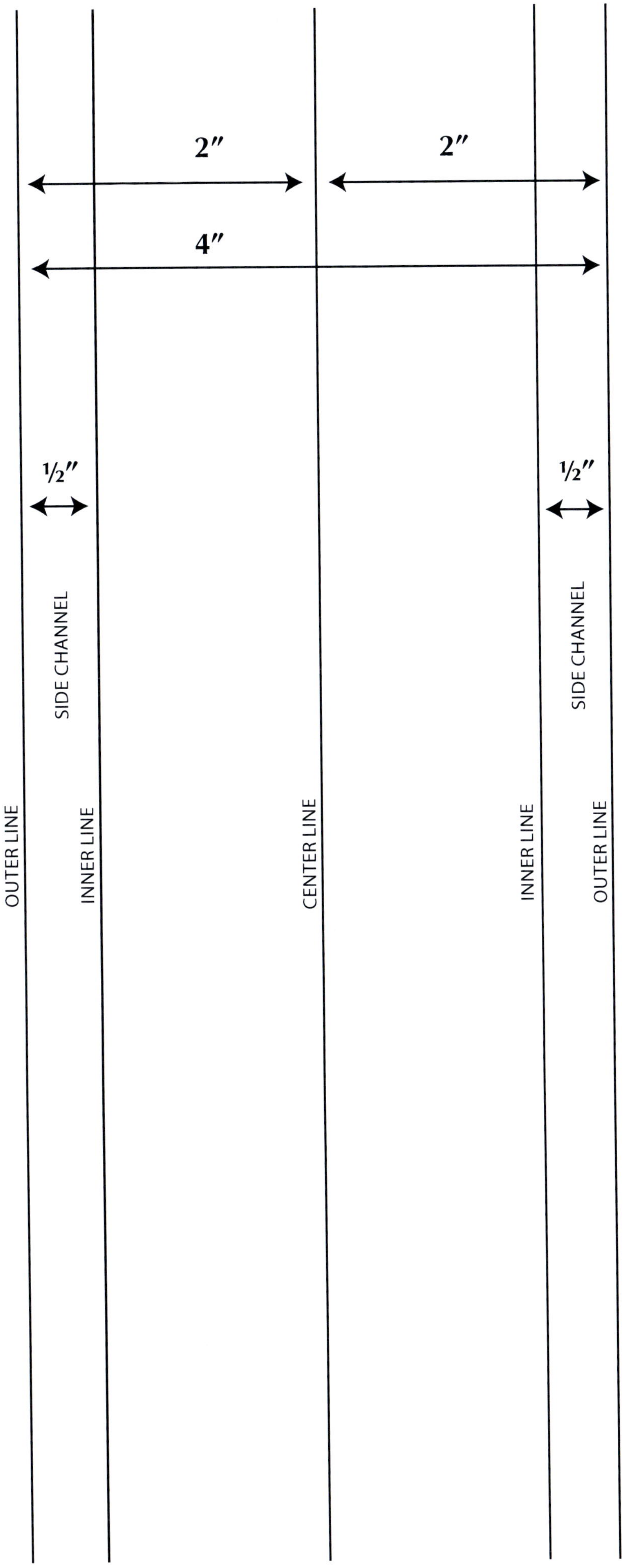

2" 2"

4"

½" ½"

SIDE CHANNEL SIDE CHANNEL

OUTER LINE

INNER LINE

CENTER LINE

INNER LINE

OUTER LINE

5. Measure the distance between the inner lines and the center line. In the diagram here, it is 1½″. (Another way to figure this distance is that it is 3 times the width of the side channel.)

6. Using that measurement, place marks along the center line that are the same distance apart. For this exercise, the marks are 1½″ apart along the center line.

7. Using a grid ruler or T-square, draw lines horizontally across the track at each mark, keeping them perpendicular to the center line. Notice that the spaces along the center line are squares, and the side channels are divided into rectangles.

8. Number the lines top to bottom, as shown.

The track is now ready for drawing the rope.

Move the tracing sheet to the next page

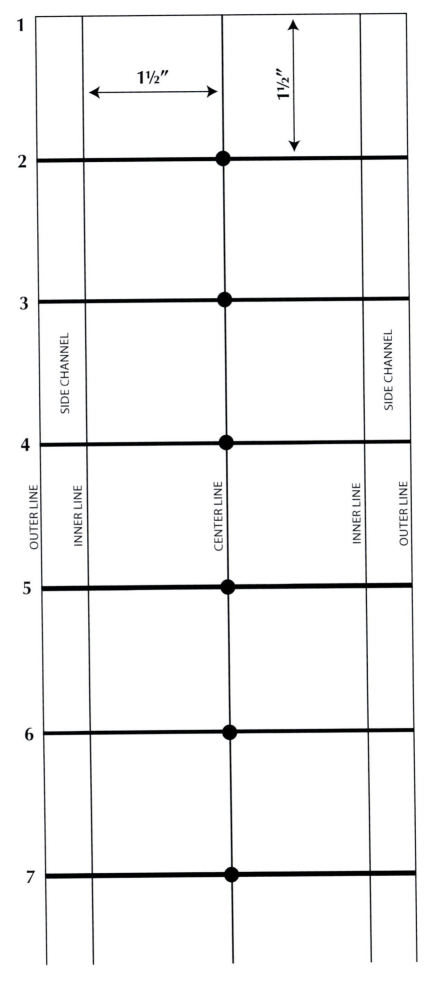

Drawing a Straight Rope   35

Drawing the rope in the track

9. Trace the curves in the rectangles of the side channels.

At odd-numbered lines the curves should touch the inside corner of the rectangle. At even-numbered lines the curves should touch the outer corner of the rectangle.

The inner points of the curves across from each other should fall on the same horizontal line, so that the pairs of curves look like parentheses.

Move the tracing sheet to the next page

A TIP FOR DRAWING CURVES

Your hands move in a curve around your wrists. Your fingers move in a similar, smaller curve from your hands. And your whole hand moves in a similar, large curve from your elbow. Whenever you draw a curve, position the paper so that the curve you are drawing arcs in the direction that your hand, wrist and arm naturally bend. The curve will be smoother and easier to draw because it fits with the natural motion of your hand, and multiple curves will be fairly consistent in size and shape.

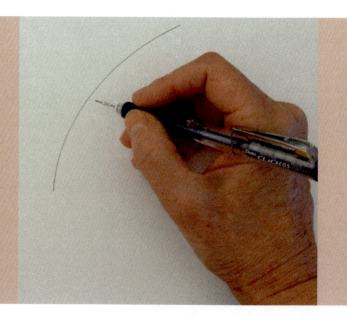

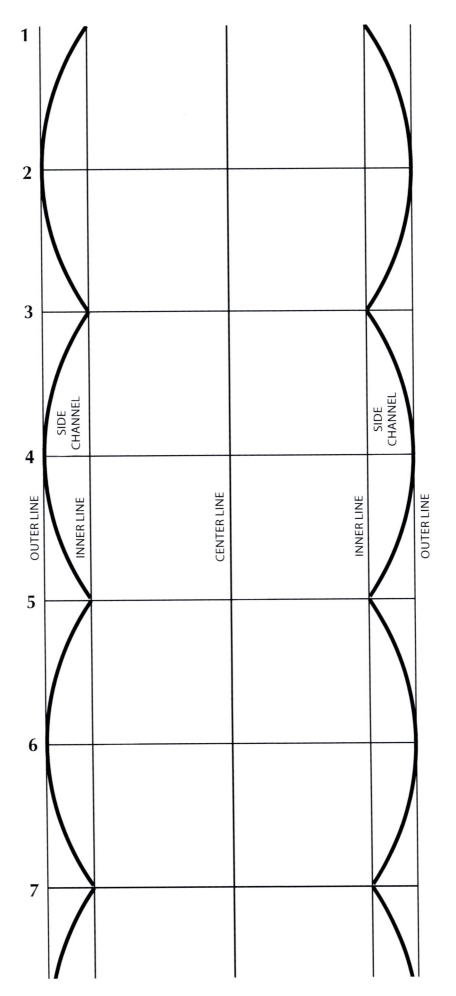

10. Draw a diagonal line (A) to connect the top inner point of a curve on the left side of the track with the bottom inner point of that curve on the right side across from it. This line passes through the crossed lines at the center of the track.

(For a rope that twists in the opposite direction, connect the diagonal lines from top right to bottom left.)

11. Using this straight diagonal line as a guide, draw a gently curving line over it (red line B). Begin by tracing the outer curve on the left of the track, pass through the crossed lines at the center of the track, and continue over the outer curve on the right side of the track. This curved line will bow slightly to each side of the diagonal line, giving the twist of the rope a graceful curve. (You might find the French curve template or the flexible curve ruler helpful for this. Also see the note on page 36 about drawing curves freehand.)

12. Trace and repeat the curved line (blue line C) for each section of the rope to keep the curves consistent throughout.

MORE TIPS FOR DRAWING CURVES

Using the wrist technique on page 36, draw the first part of the curve up to the center line, then turn the paper and draw the second part of the curve. This lets you draw both parts of the curve using the same natural curve of your hand.

Draw half of the curve up to the middle line, then trace it and copy it on the other side of the track to complete the curve. This will ensure that the second part of the curve is an exact match to the first part.

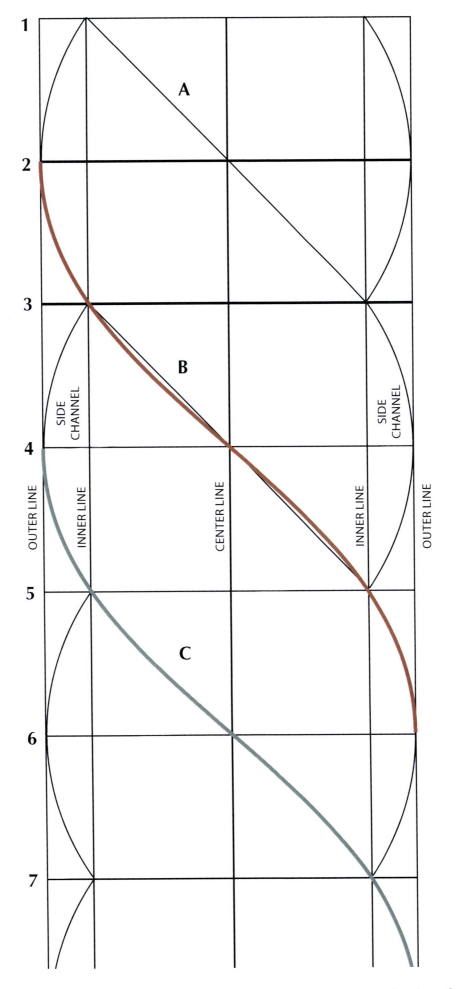

Drawing a Straight Rope   **39**

Drawing a Rope - Corners

If you want to carry your rope around a corner, here are several ways to do it. Place your tracing sheet over the grid at right to try out these corner configurations or to create new ones of your own.

This elegant corner changes the direction of the rope as it turns from side to bottom. If you want to change directions in mid-side, use the configuration below.

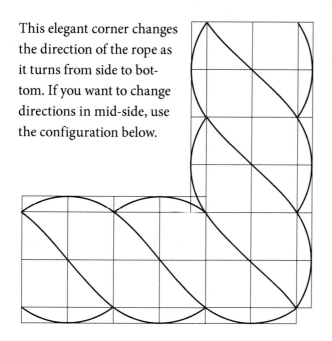

This configuration keeps the rope twisting in the same direction as it turns the corner.

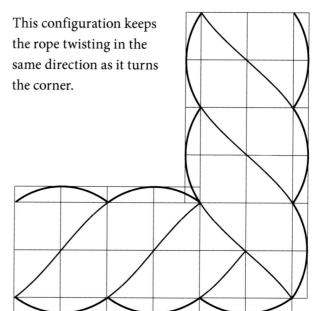

Use this configuration to change direction in mid-side. Place it at center top or bottom of a border to create symmetry. Erase one or both or neither of the dashed lines, as suits your design.

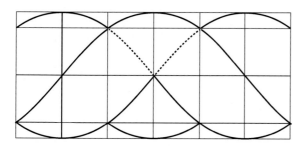

This "clubbed" rope seems to tie off the side rope and then re-start a new rope along the bottom. It keeps the rope twisting in the same direction.

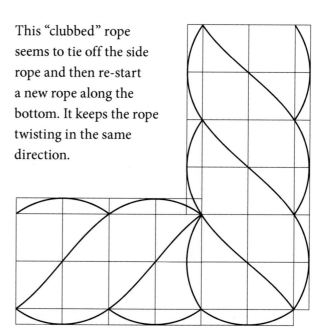

Drawing a Curved Rope

Drawing a curved rope is almost the same as straight—set up a track and draw the rope in it. You'll just have to be a little more adaptable with the curves.

WHAT YOU'LL NEED

- A tracing sheet (clear plastic page protector or tracing paper)
- A dry-erase marker (for a page protector) or a pencil (for tracing paper)
- For erasing: A tissue (for a page protector) or an eraser (for tracing paper)
- A clear ruler with a grid (like a rotary-cutting ruler) or a T-square
- Optional: A flexible curve ruler or French curve template (shown on page 18)

STEPS

Lay the tracing sheet over the page at right.

Setting up the track

1. Trace the Center Line. This is where the center of the rope will be.

2. Trace the two Outer Lines—they are parallel to the center line on each side. These are the outside edges of the rope.

When drawing your own rope, use the grid ruler or T-square to plot the outer lines (the blue rectangle in the diagram at right). Place it perpendicular to the center line to mark dots plotting the line, then connect the dots, either freehand or with the flexible curve ruler. The rope can be any width you want. (See tips for drawing curves on pages 36 and 38.)

3. Measure between the outer lines and divide the distance by 8. This is the Side Channel Width. (In this example the width between the outer lines is 3″ so the side channel width is ⅜″. This distance may vary slightly because of the curves.)

4. Trace the Inner Lines. To find their placement, measure the side channel width inward from the outer lines and draw them parallel to the outer lines. (You will probably be able to draw these freehand after placing a few marks to guide you.) In the example here, the inner lines are ⅜″ inside the outer lines. The outer lines and the inner lines create the side channel.

Move the tracing sheet to the next page

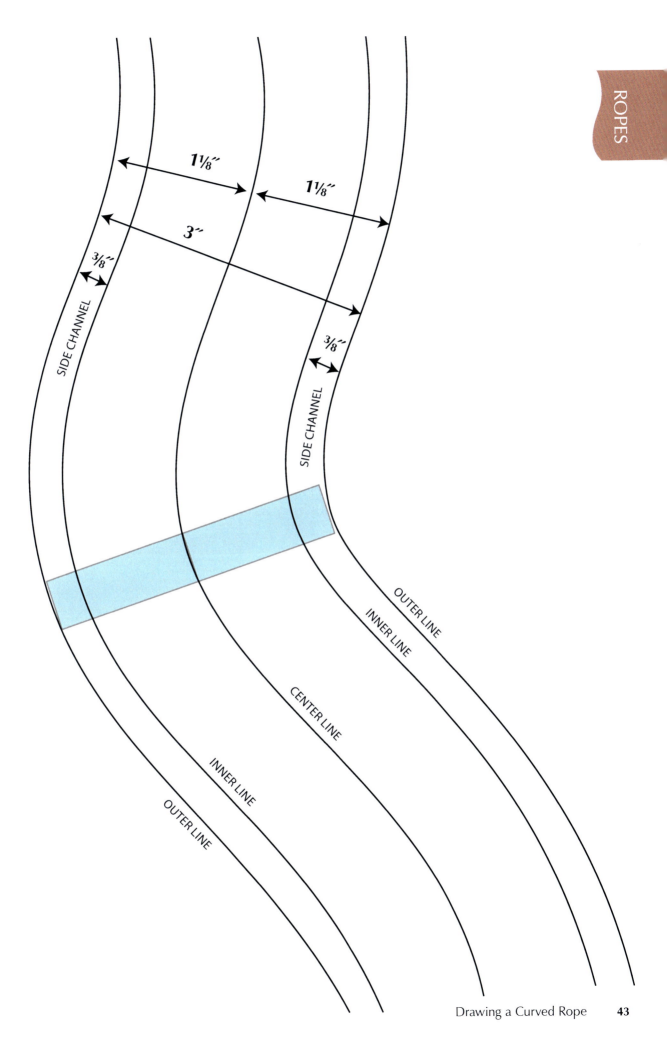

1⅛″

1⅛″

3″

3⁄8″

3⁄8″

SIDE CHANNEL

SIDE CHANNEL

OUTER LINE

INNER LINE

CENTER LINE

INNER LINE

OUTER LINE

Drawing a Curved Rope   **43**

5. Measure the distance between the inner lines and the center line. In the diagram here it is 1⅛″. (Another way to figure this distance is that it is 3 times the width of the side channels.)

6. Using that measurement, place marks this distance apart along the center line. Here, the marks are 1⅛″ apart.

7. Using the grid ruler or T-square, draw crossing lines through the marks on the center line, extending to the outer lines to create a track. As you did in Step 2, keep the ruler perpendicular to the center line.

Notice that even though the spaces along the center line are equal, when the crossing lines touch the outer lines the distances between them are different.

8. Number the crossing lines from top to bottom.

The track is now ready for drawing the rope.

Move the tracing sheet to the next page ➡

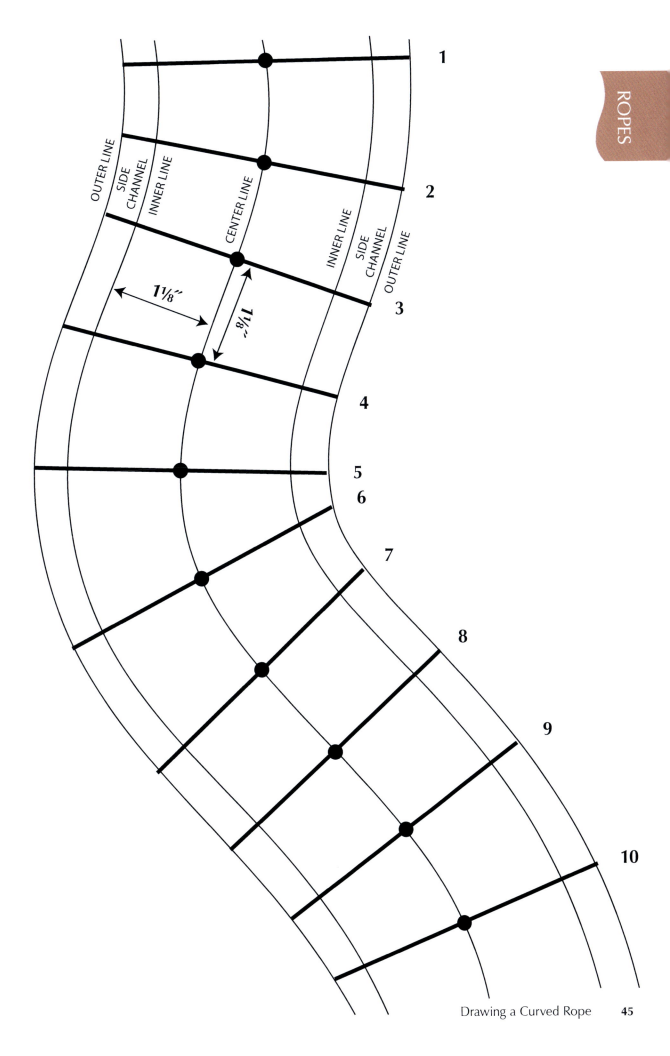

1

2

OUTER LINE
SIDE CHANNEL
INNER LINE

CENTER LINE

INNER LINE
SIDE CHANNEL
OUTER LINE

3

1⅛″

1⅛″

4

5

6

7

8

9

10

Drawing a Curved Rope   **45**

Drawing the rope

9. Trace the curves in each pair of rectangles in the side channels.

At odd-numbered crossing lines the curves should touch the inside corner of the rectangle, and at even-numbered crossing lines the curves should touch the outer corner of the rectangle.

The inner part of the curves on opposite sides should fall on the same line so that the pairs of curves look like parentheses.

(This looks rather like a caterpillar, doesn't it?!)

Move the tracing sheet to the next page ➡

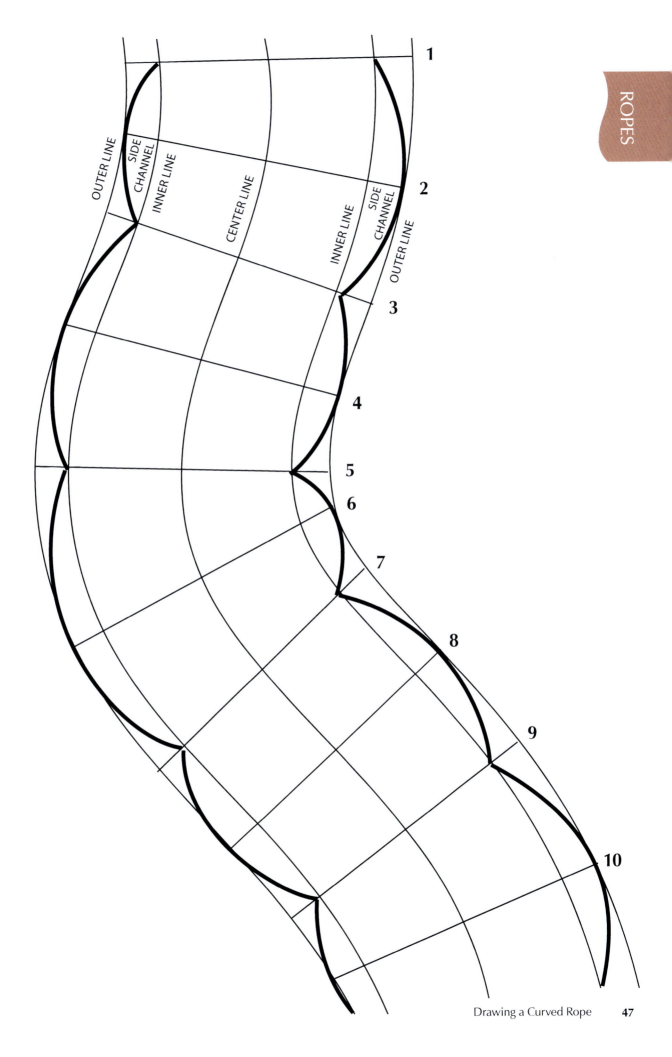

1

OUTER LINE

SIDE
CHANNEL

INNER LINE

CENTER LINE

INNER LINE

SIDE
CHANNEL

OUTER LINE

2

3

4

5

6

7

8

9

10

Drawing a Curved Rope   **47**

10. Trace a diagonal line (A) to connect the top inner point of a curve on the left side of the track with the bottom inner point of the curve on the right side directly across from it. Unlike in the straight rope, this line may or may not pass through the point where the center line and the crossing line intersect. Because the track is curved, sometimes these diagonal lines will pass through the crossed lines at the center of the track (blue line B2) and sometimes they won't (A and red line B1).

(To draw a rope that twists in the reverse direction, connect the diagonal lines from upper right to lower left.)

11. Using the diagonal lines as guides, draw curving lines (B1 and B2) from side to side in the track. Begin by tracing the outer curve in the left side channel, continue the curve to the center line, then curve in the opposite direction and continue tracing over the outer curve in the right channel. These curved lines will bow to each side of the diagonal line, giving the twist a graceful curve. Notice that where there is more curve in the track, the most graceful curve might swing quite wide of the diagonal line. Because the track is curved, each curve will be different.

The track will help you draw the curves freehand, but if you want help, use a flexible curve ruler or a French curve template. Make each curve as smooth and graceful as you can. See tips for drawing curves on pages 36 and 38.

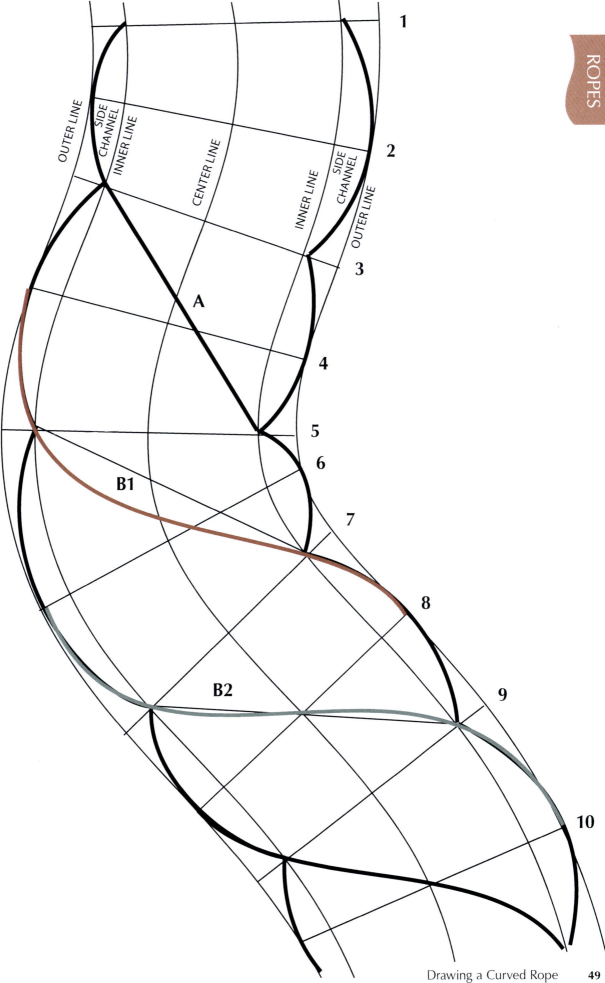

1

OUTER LINE
SIDE CHANNEL
INNER LINE

CENTER LINE

INNER LINE
SIDE CHANNEL
OUTER LINE

2

3

A

4

5

6

B1

7

8

B2

9

10

Drawing a Rope Ring

Drawing a rope ring is easy—just set up the track as a circle.

WHAT YOU'LL NEED

- A ruler large enough to cross your circle
- A tracing sheet (clear plastic page protector or tracing paper)
- A dry-erase marker (for a page protector) or a pencil (for tracing paper)
- A tissue (for dry-erase markers) or an eraser (for pencil)
- Optional: A flexible curve ruler or French curve template (shown on page 18)

Optional for this exercise, but necessary for drawing your own:

- A drawing compass (for making circles) and a protractor

STEPS

Lay the tracing sheet over the page at right and trace the diagram as you follow the steps below.

Setting up the track

1. Draw the Outer Circle (A).

2. Draw the Inner Circle (B). (All circles use the same center point.)

The distance between the outer circle (A) and the inner circle (B) is the width of the rope.

The distance from the center point to the inner circle is the Inner Radius.

The width of the rope divided by 8 is the Channel Width.

3. Draw the Center Circle (C). The radius of the center circle is the inner radius plus half the width of the rope.

4. Draw the Inner Channel Circle (D). The radius of the inner channel circle is the inner radius plus the channel width (⅛ of the width of the rope).

5. Draw the Outer Channel Circle (E). The radius of the outer channel circle is the outer circle radius minus the channel width (⅛ of the width of the rope).

6. Draw the Vertical Axis (F) all the way cross the circles, through the center point.

7. Draw the Horizontal Axis (G) perpendicular to the vertical axis, through the center point.

8. Draw diagonal lines (H and I) at 45 degree angles to (F) and (G), through the center point.

9. Continue drawing other diagonal lines to divide in half the spaces between existing diagonal lines. Always pass through the center point of the circle (J, K, L, M) so you have an even number of divisions.

Move the tracing sheet to the next page

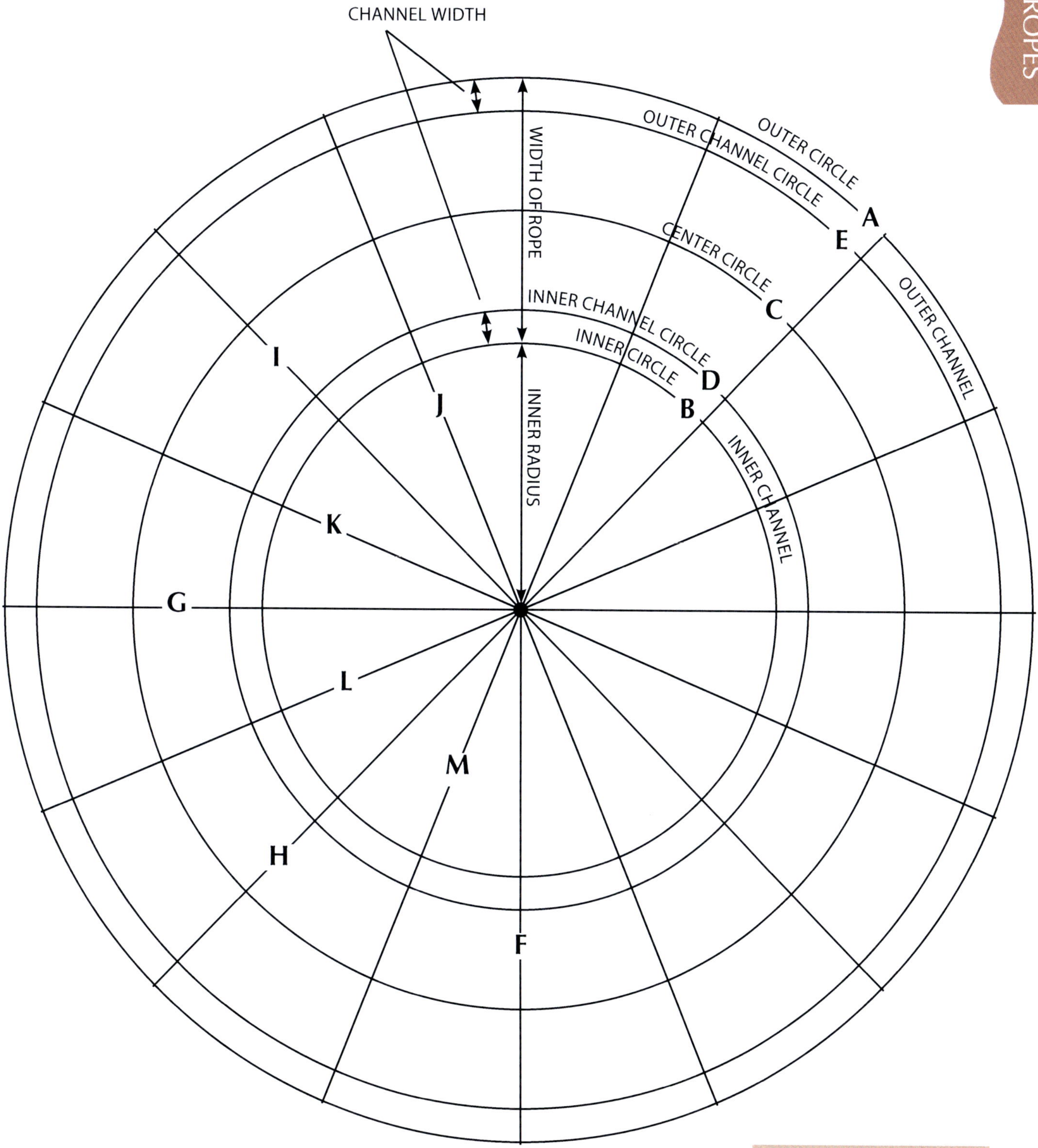

CHANNEL WIDTH

WIDTH OF ROPE

OUTER CIRCLE

OUTER CHANNEL CIRCLE

CENTER CIRCLE

INNER CHANNEL CIRCLE

INNER CIRCLE

OUTER CHANNEL

INNER CHANNEL

INNER RADIUS

A

E

C

D

B

I

J

K

G

L

M

H

F

4 RADII: 90 degrees
8 RADII: 45 degrees
16 RADII: 22.5 degrees
32 RADII: 11.25 degrees
64 RADII: 5.625 degrees

Drawing a Rope Ring   51

Drawing the rope

10. Draw the curves in the inner and outer channels (A1, A2, A3, A4, continue around the ring).

The inner points of the curves in both channels should fall on the same line, so that the pairs of curves look like parentheses.

11. Connect one pair of inner and outer curves with a curved line that goes from upper left to lower right and passes through the crossed lines at the center circle (B). It helps to rotate the paper so that the pair of curves you are working on is always at the top of the circle. (See pages 36 and 38 for tips on drawing curves.)

For a rope that twists in the opposite direction, connect the diagonal lines from top right to bottom left.

12. Using this line as a guide, smooth out the curve from the outer circle to the inner circle (C).

13. Trace and repeat this curve to create all the other rope sections around the ring (D).

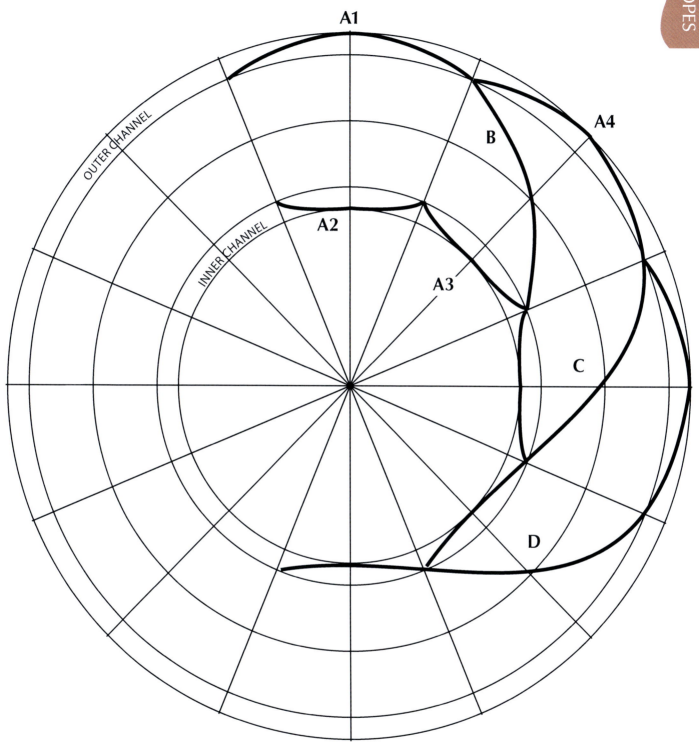

A1

A2

A3

A4

B

C

D

OUTER CHANNEL

INNER CHANNEL

SURPRISE!
Designed, sewn and quilted
by Barbara Shirley
35″ x 47″

Barbara took the idea of ribbons literally to make curled ribbons on a present. The ribbon coils were appliquéd by hand over a pieced background. The back of the quilt is the opened box—see what was in it on page 161.

CHAPTER 3

Ribbons

Think about a ribbon and how it bends: it curls to make a coil or it bends back and forth to make a wave. Waves and coils show up in curling ribbon on a package. Ringlets in a girl's hair. The ribbons of a ballerina shoe. A ribbon dancer's acrobatics. They can be used in quilt designs to represent these things pictorially, or simply as elegant geometric forms.

Just as in drawing a rope, the process of drawing ribbons is made simple by drawing in a track. The track can be straight or curved, and the outside lines of the track can be parallel or can vary in width. For ribbons, the track is also an important part of the assembly process.

The first two steps of drawing a ribbon—setting up the track and plotting the curves—are the same for all ribbons. After the curves are drawn, simply erase different sections of the lines to form either a wave or a coil.

The next few pages are set up so that you can trace each page step-by-step to set up a track and draw a wave or coil in it. Place a clear plastic page protector over the first page and trace it with a dry erase marker. Move the page protector to the next page and the next, tracing each page according to the instructions on that page.

When you are ready to draft a ribbon for your own quilt design, set up a track with your own measurements and draw your own ribbon in the size and shape that fit your design.

Gallery
of Ribbon Quilts

PARTY SQUARE

Designed, pieced, hand appliquéd and quilted
by Nienke Smit
40" x 40"

Despite its carefully-arranged structure, this quilt is bursting with energy. The careful placement of light, medium and dark values of the hand-dyed fabric emphasizes the illusion of three dimensions in each ribbon.

Two different takes on a ribbon dancer show how beautifully realistic and flowing ribbons can be in a quilt.

RIBBON DANCER
Designed, sewn and quilted
by Linda Ward
33½" x 33"

"This is my daughter's silhouette – who knew all those ballet lessons would come in handy for quilting!!" Appliquéd and pieced in hand-dyed cotton fabrics.

RIBBON DANCER
Designed, sewn and quilted by Devi Lanphere
62" x 40"

The flying ribbons, appliquéd in hand-dyed cotton fabrics, truly embody Devi's free spirit. The blue pattern behind the ribbons is a sheer drapery fabric overlaying the white background.

SPIRALING RIBBONS

Designed, sewn and quilted
by Maureen Czerneda
24" x 26"

Single coils appliquéd by hand
imitate those pesky threads and
ribbons that never seem to stay
on the spool!

LET'S GO FLY A KITE

Designed, sewn and quilted
by Mavis Abbey
30½" x 51½"

Three colorful kites sport
festive ribbon tails. The red
kite is decorated with a
Baravelle spiral and the blue
kite with two sections of a
spiral mandala (see page 164).

These two quilters took the notion of a ribbon wave literally and used it to create ocean waves.

ACCIDENTAL LANDSCAPE
Designed, sewn and quilted
by Priscilla Roehm
23" x 23"

Priscilla used hand-dyed fabrics to create a soft sunset and eyelash yarn for seaweed. She even appliquéd batting for the mist off the wave.

SEA YOU AT THE BEACH
Designed and sewn
by Claire Beebe
Quilted by Lori Kukuk
46½" x 46½"

Waves and coils can be found all over this beach—the waves, the sun's rays, the clouds and the frame. A spiral block makes the sail of the boat. (Claire was 12 when she made this.)

MERRY CHRISTMAS
Designed by Deborah Rice and Leslie Arbuckle,
sewn and quilted by Leslie Arbuckle
34½" x 53"

Instead of being the garland *on* the Christmas tree, this single coiling ribbon *is* the tree. "Merry Christmas" is spelled out in a spiral chain at the top of the quilt.

UNRULY ORNAMENTS
Designed, sewn and quilted by Mona Beck
40½" x 40½"

A double coil in a circle forms an elegant wreath, while appliquéd ornaments express a rather more raucous view of a holiday celebration!

Tangled ribbons, in one quilt coming apart, in the other coming together.

HEARTSTRINGS
Designed, sewn and quilted
by Debra Reinert
25½" x 25½"

Notice the many layers and textures of this design—two tightly bent waves against two gently curving ribbons in the background. Waves appliquéd in a track, then pieced into the quilt.

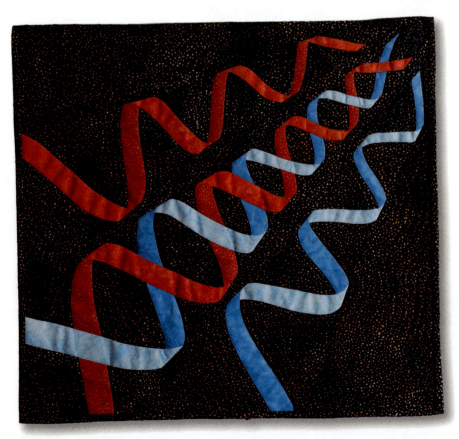

MEDIATION
Designed and quilted
by Barbara Mahaffy
21" x 19"

Two single waves intertwine to form a double wave. Light and dark values in two colors keep the ribbons clearly defined. Hand appliquéd ribbons, machine quilted.

INSPIRED BY TIFFANY
Designed, sewn and quilted
by Darlene Folk
19½" x 19½"

You can almost miss the
double coil in this quilt—it's
just a small one forming the
vase. But the ribbon theme
continues with actual ribbon
appliquéd in the border.

UNTITLED
Designed, sewn and quilted
by Mary Schwartz
44" x 44"

A double coil forms a
dramatic border for this
quilt, while also framing the
corner blocks quite nicely.
The square around the center
spiral also appears as if made
of woven ribbons.

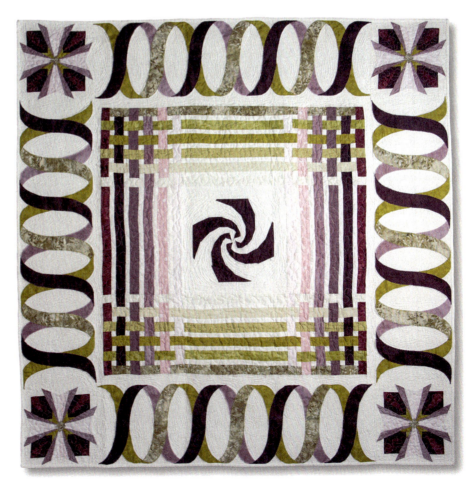

DISCOVERY

Designed, sewn and quilted
by Michael Gustafson
33" x 38½"

Michael makes imaginative
use of single coiled ribbons
for the hair of the mermaid
and double waves for the
water. Raw-edge appliqué.

MOONLIGHT

Designed, sewn and quilted
by Michael Gustafson
27" x 33"

More imaginative ribbons
—here, double ribbons in
the open peacock tail, single
ribbons in the hanging tail,
and even double ribbons to
create the texture of the bark
on the tree limb.
Raw-edge appliqué.

**COLOURED RIBBONS
IN THE MOON LIGHT**
Designed, sewn and quilted by
Sherrie Tyzzer Jewson
32" x 53"

These stunning ribbons were created in hand-colored silk. Just as remarkable was the way it was constructed. Each piece of ribbon was individually quilted and bound. The pieces were attached to their tracks which were then quilted and bound. Finally, the tracks were attached to the black background and that was quilted and bound.

RASPBERRY MINUET

Designed, sewn and quilted
by Julie Perkins
34½" x 35"

This unusual kaleidoscope quilt uses tightly twisted ribbons for the flower and more gently twisted ribbons for the leaves. Take a close look at the quilting where you'll find the same motifs repeated. Hand appliqué.

Two quilts combine ribbons and flowers in uniquely different ways

TRILLIUM HOPE

Designed, sewn and quilted
by Jane Hellwege
35" x 41"

With its grid-like brown background, ribbons, and rounded shape, this quilt makes me think of a basket of flowers. Just the right difference in value on the ribbons gives them a perfect feeling of three dimensions. Hand appliqué.

SPRING FLING
Designed, hand-pieced, hand-appliquéd,
hand-quilted by Jackie Simpson
61" x 62½"

The colors of spring grace this quilt that combines single and double coiled ribbons, stars, and a spiral mandala center. Hand appliquéd and hand quilted.

TU TU MUCH
Designed, sewn and quilted
by Mary Dufur
34½" x 34½"

This poor octopus—I laugh every time I look at this quilt! Aside from the adorable design, notice that even though the ribbons are single, they are placed on the legs at an angle that suggests double ribbons wrapped around the legs. Raw-edge machine appliqué with satin-stitched edges

LIONESQUE ILLUSION
Designed and sewn
by Kathy Radl and Ann White
Quilted by Krissy Brawner
34½″ x 34½″

The stylized mane of coiled ribbons is just one of the beauties of this wonderful quilt. Take time to look carefully at the masterful shading of the face and the soulful beaded eyes. Raw-edge appliqué.

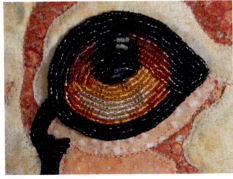

SCRAPBOX EXPLOSION
Designed, sewn and quilted
by Linda Upp
41" diameter

Fireworks of coiling ribbons in rainbow colors not only won awards for this quilt, it was also chosen as the theme image for the following year's show. Linda got to see it on billboards all over the county! Raw-edge appliqué.

LACY SPIRALS
Designed, sewn and quilted
by Nienke Smit
38" x 45"

The coiled ribbons in this very modern quilt are made with an unusual material: lace. Raw-edge appliqué with satin stitched edges

Drawing a Ribbon

Just as with drawing a rope, a ribbon is drawn in a track. When its time to sew the ribbon, the track becomes an important part of the construction.

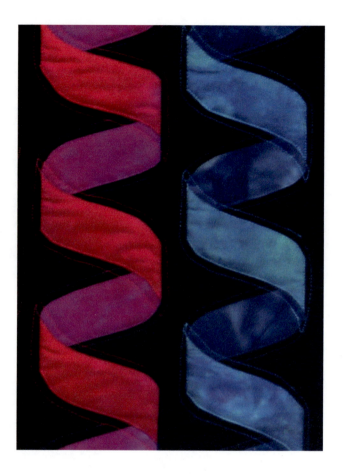

WHAT YOU'LL NEED:

- A tracing sheet (clear plastic page protector or tracing paper)
- A dry-erase marker (for a page protector or a pencil (for tracing paper)
- For erasing: Cotton swabs (for a page protector) or an eraser (for tracing paper)
- A ruler or straightedge
- A flexible curve ruler or French curve template (see page 18)

STEPS

Lay the tracing sheet over the page at right.

1. Trace the two parallel lines to set up the track. The width between them should be the width you want the finished ribbon to be.

2. Trace the red line to draw a curved line from side to side in the track, touching each track line as it curves.

3. Trace the blue line to make a second curve parallel to the first one.

Move the tracing sheet to the next page

WHEN YOU DRAW YOUR OWN

- Use a flexible curve ruler or a French curve template for help with drawing curves (see page 18).

- To make the second curved line, move the page protector or tracing paper up or down the track and trace the first curved line again.

- The curves of the ribbon do not all have to be the same. But if you do want them to be the same, draw the first curve in the track, then trace that segment for each repetition of the curve.

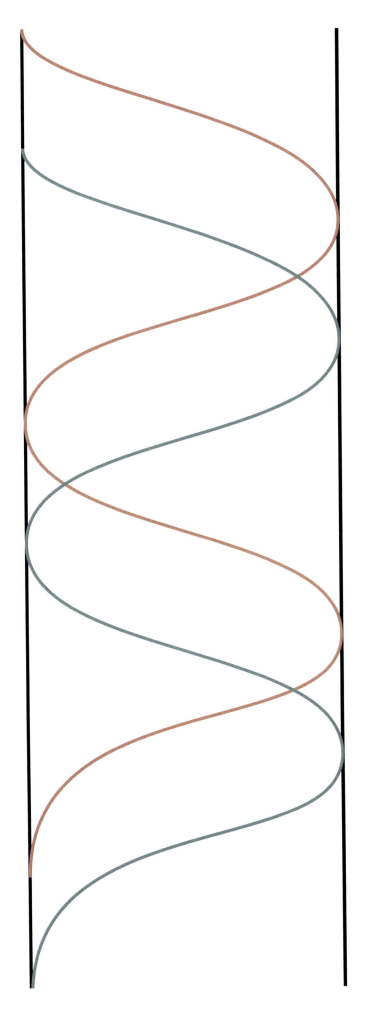

This is the step where you make the ribbon into either a wave or a coil.

FOR A WAVE

1. Notice that the two curved lines intersect each time they come close to the track. Between that intersection and the sides of the track, erase the *top* sections of line (red dashed lines "A" at right, diagram A below).

2. To wave in the opposite direction, erase the *bottom* sections of the curved line between each intersection and the track (blue dashed lines "B" at right, diagram B below).

3. To emphasize the three-dimensional effect of the ribbon, make the "front" or "outside" of the ribbon lighter and the "back" or "inside" of the ribbon darker. You can also add shading inside the bends where a shadow might occur.

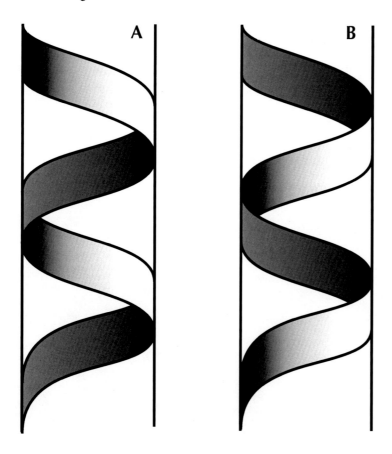

Move the tracing sheet to the next page ➔

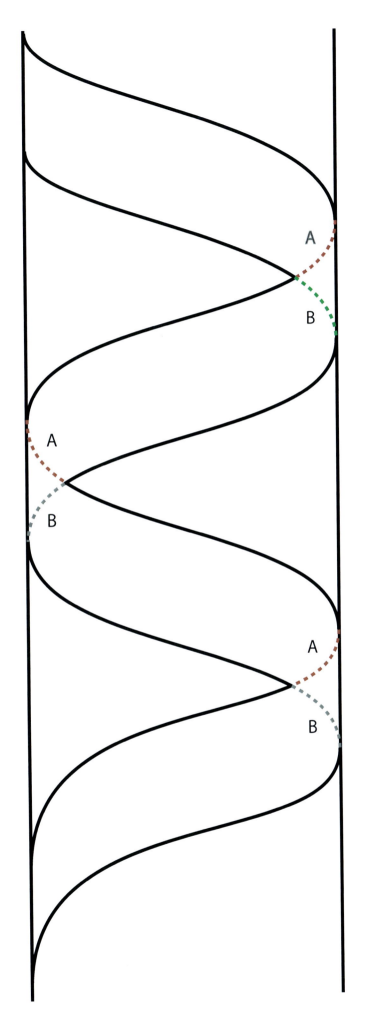

DRAWING A STRAIGHT RIBBON - CONTINUED

FOR A COIL

1. Notice that the two curved lines intersect each time they come close to the track. Between the intersection and the outer line on the *right* side of the track, erase the *top* sections of line. Between the intersection and the outer line on the *left* side of the track, erase the *bottom* sections of line (blue dashed lines "C" at right, diagram C below).

2. To make the coil spin in the opposite direction: Between the intersection and the outer line on the *right* side of the track erase the *bottom* section of line. Between the intersections and the outer line on the *left* side of the track, erase the *top* section of line (red dashed lines "D" at right, diagram D below).

3. To emphasize the three-dimension effect of the ribbon, make the "front" or "outside" of the ribbon lighter and the "back" or "inside" of the ribbon darker. You can also add shading in the bends where a shadow might be.

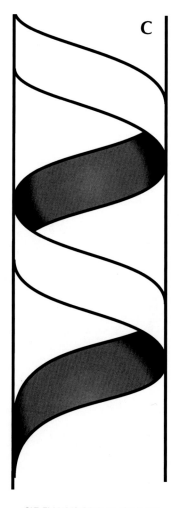

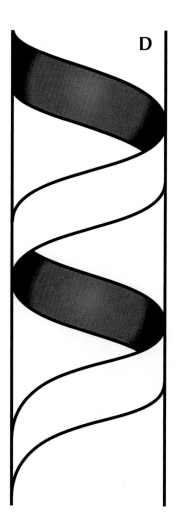

76   SIDEWAYS SPIRAL QUILTS

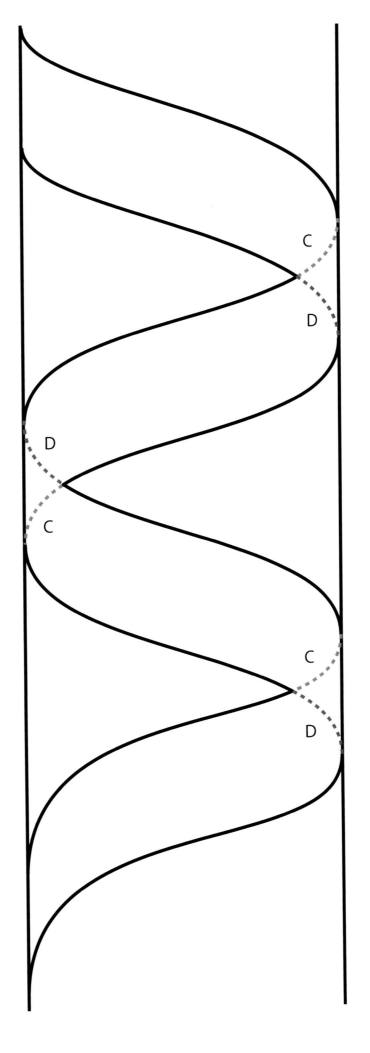

Drawing a Ribbon - Corners

To make a ribbon turn a corner, draw one long loop into the corner, and one short loop that crosses below it. Place your tracing sheet over the diagram here to learn how, then try your own.

1. Draw a vertical track and a horizontal track. Intersect the lines to form a corner box. In the corner box, draw a diagonal line from the inner corner to the outer corner.

2. Draw ribbons in the vertical and horizontal tracks according to the instructions on the previous pages. The ribbons must end on the inner side of the track before the corner (A1, B1, A2, B2). The stopping point for the ribbon closest to the corner should be at least the width of the ribbon. (RW = the width of the ribbon measured parallel to the track).

3. In the corner box, place marks on the outer track line about ⅓ of the distance from the corner (C1, C2).

4. In the corner box, place marks on the inside of the square about 1/3 of the distance down from the outer track line (D1, D2).

5. Long loop (red line): Starting at the end of the ribbon line closest to the corner box (A1), draw a curve from the end of the ribbon line, up to C1, around to C2, and end at A2.

6. Starting from where the red line crosses the diagonal line in the corner (E1), measure RW toward the center and place a dot on the diagonal line (E2).

7. Short loop (blue line): Starting at B1, draw a curve from the end of the ribbon line, up to D1, through E2, around to D2, and end at B2.

8. Bent edge of ribbon (purple lines): Draw lines from D1 toward C1 and from D2 toward C2.

9. Find the intersections of the curved lines by the blue lines (F1, F2). Erase either the red dashed section of line or the blue dashed section of line (see diagrams below).

For yet another way to turn a corner, look at the end loops of *I Love You to Infinity* on page 159.

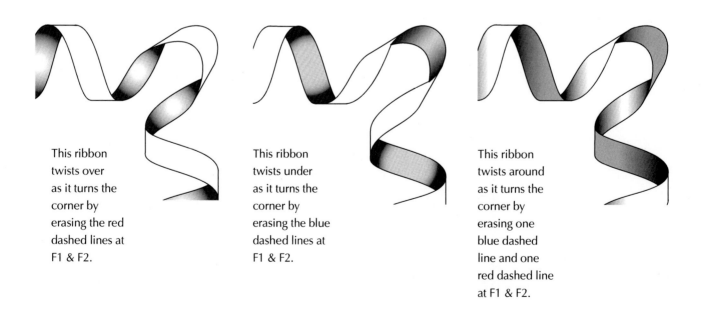

This ribbon twists over as it turns the corner by erasing the red dashed lines at F1 & F2.

This ribbon twists under as it turns the corner by erasing the blue dashed lines at F1 & F2.

This ribbon twists around as it turns the corner by erasing one blue dashed line and one red dashed line at F1 & F2.

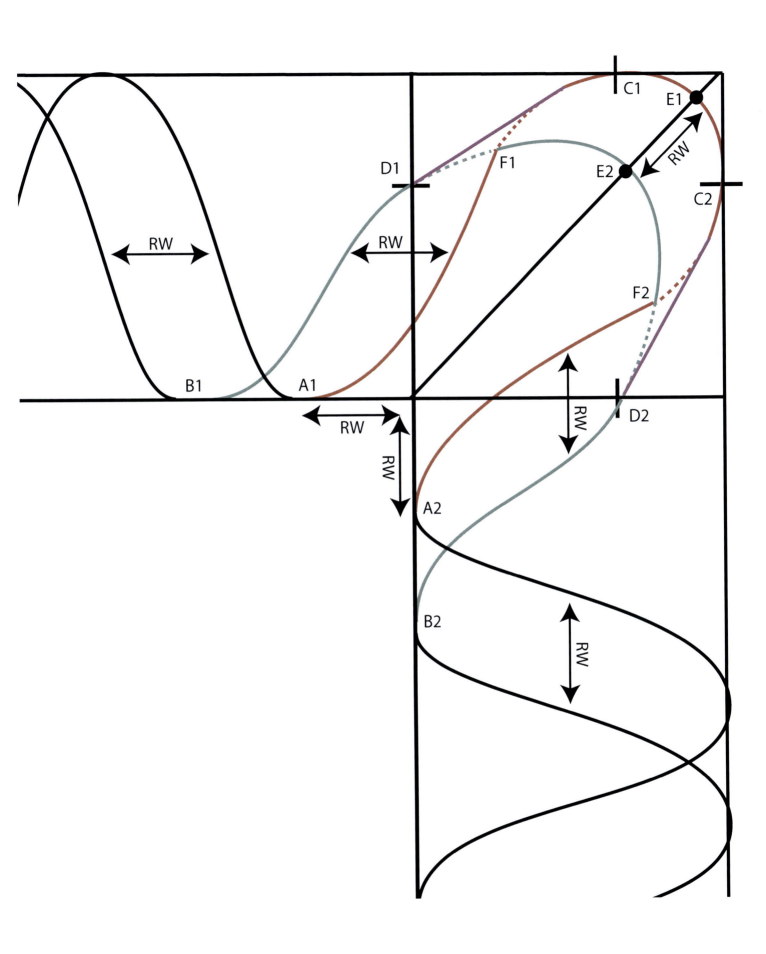

Drawing a Curved Ribbon

The same steps that you used to draw a straight ribbon can also be used to draw curved ribbons—just start with a curved track.

WHAT YOU'LL NEED:

- A tracing sheet (clear plastic page protector or tracing paper)
- A dry-erase marker (for a page protector or a pencil (for tracing paper)
- For erasing: Cotton swabs (for a page protector) or an eraser (for tracing paper)
- A flexible curve ruler or French curve template (see page 18)

STEPS

Lay the tracing sheet over the page at right.

1. Trace the two black lines to set up the track. The width between them should be the width you want the finished ribbon to be. The width can vary.

2. Trace the red line to draw a curved line from side to side in the track, touching each track line as it curves.

3. Trace the blue line to draw a second curved line more or less parallel to the first one.

4. Notice that the red and blue lines intersect each time they come close to the track. Between that intersection and the edge of the track, erase the dashed sections of line to create a wave (see page 74) or a coil (see page 76).

WHEN YOU DRAW YOUR OWN

To make the second curved line, trace an individual segment of the first curved line from one side of the track to the other. Move the page protector or tracing paper up or down the track and copy that segment parallel to the first line. Repeat for each segment of the curve. Draw freehand to fill in any gaps in the second line.

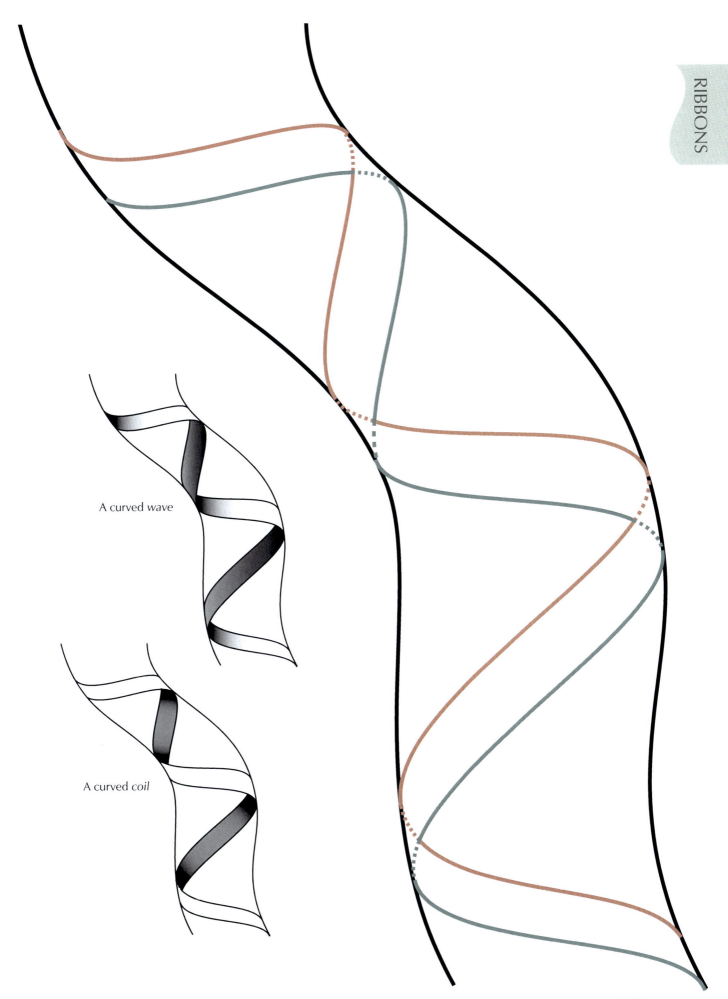

A curved *wave*

A curved *coil*

Drawing a Curved Ribbon   81

Drawing Double Ribbons

Create double waves or double coils just by drawing two ribbons in the same track. When you draw the first ribbon, leave enough space between each curve to fit in the second ribbon. In a straight track, you can draw the second ribbon by tracing the first ribbon. In a curved track, you will need to draw the second ribbon from scratch (see page 80).

After creating the second ribbon, you will see that the two ribbons cross in the middle of the track. At each crossing, decide which ribbon will pass over the other and erase the corresponding sections of the lines. You can create a wide variety of interwoven and layered effects simply by changing which ribbon lays on top of the crossover, and by changing the directions of the waves or coils. Experiment until you get an effect you like.

WHAT YOU'LL NEED:

- A tracing sheet (clear plastic page protector or tracing paper)
- A dry-erase marker (for a page protector or a pencil (for tracing paper)
- For erasing: Cotton swabs (for a page protector) or an eraser (for tracing paper)
- A ruler or straightedge
- A flexible curve ruler or French curve template (see page 18)

STEPS

Lay the tracing sheet over the page at right.

1. Trace the two black lines to set up the track. The width between them should be the width you want the finished ribbon to be.

2. Draw the first ribbon by tracing the red lines. (The process is the same for creating a single ribbon on page 72.)

3. Draw the second ribbon by tracing the blue lines. Notice that where the red ribbon curved to the left, the blue ribbon curves to the right. (Repeat the process for creating a single ribbon.)

4. Erase dashed lines in each ribbon at the sides of the track to create waves (see page 74) or coils (see page 76).

5. Erase either the red dashed lines or the blue dashed lines at each crossover in the center of the track to make one ribbon pass over the other (turn the page for examples).

Continue to the next page ➡

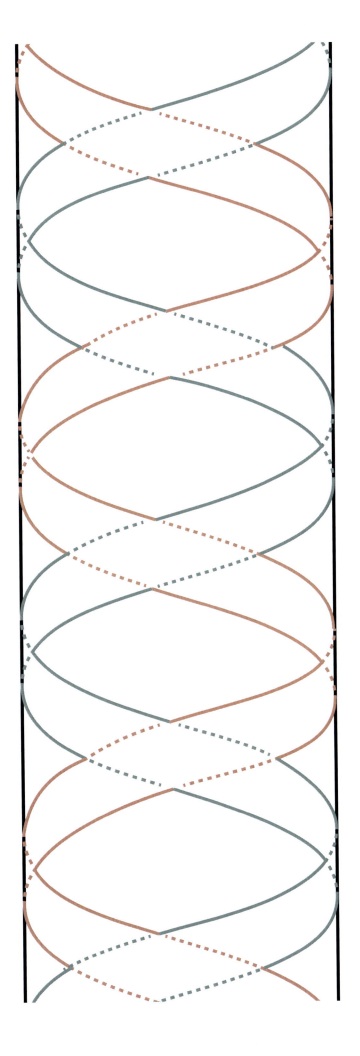

Here are three versions of a double wave or coil. Each began with the same track and ribbons; the only differences are which direction the ribbons bend (look at the over/under at the edges of the tracks) and which ribbon crosses over the other in the middle of the track. To see the differences clearly, try tracing each example, or recreate them from the diagram on the previous page.

 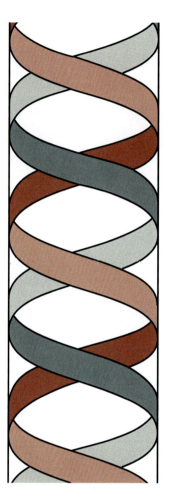 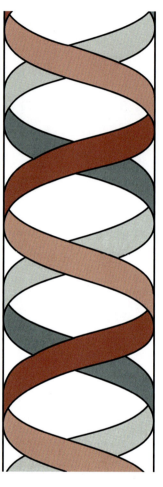

A. In this double *coil*, the two ribbons coil in opposite directions and the blue ribbon lies entirely inside the red ribbon.

B. In this double *wave*, the two ribbons wave in the same direction and intertwine. (The center crossovers are the same as at left, but the bends at the track edges are different.)

C. In this double wave, the two ribbons bend in the same direction, and the second ribbon sits completely behind the first ribbon.

In reality, you are not limited to two ribbons. You could create as many ribbons—in as many colors—as you want. Let your imagination and your creativity run wild!

Intertwining double ribbons works with curved ribbons just as well as with straight ones. The ribbons in each drawing on this page are arranged in the same way as the drawings on the left page.

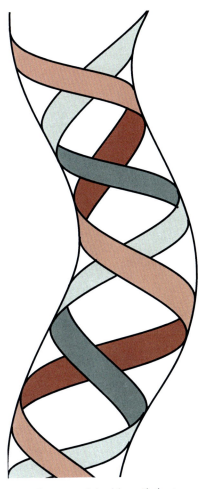

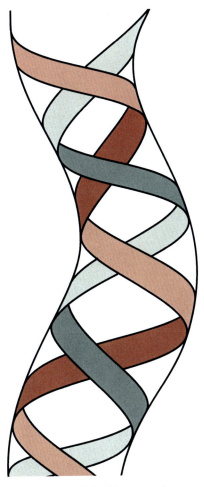

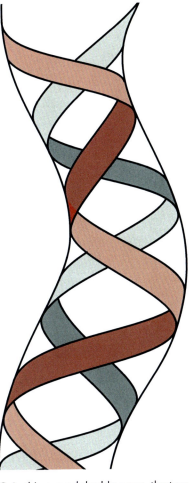

A. In this curved double *coil,* the two ribbons twist in opposite directions and the blue ribbon lies entirely inside the red ribbon.

B. In this curved double *wave,* the two ribbons wave in the same direction and intertwine. (The center crossovers are the same as at left, but the bends at the track edges are different.)

C. In this curved double wave, the two ribbons bend in the same direction, and the second ribbon sits completely behind the first ribbon.

Drawing a Ribbon Ring

Drawing a ribbon ring is easy—just set up the track as a circle.

WHAT YOU'LL NEED

- A ruler large enough to cross your circle
- A tracing sheet (clear plastic page protector or tracing paper)
- A dry-erase marker (for a page protector) or a pencil (for tracing paper)
- A tissue (for dry-erase markers) or an eraser (for pencil)
- Optional: A flexible curve ruler or French curve template (shown on page 18)

Optional for this exercise, but necessary for drawing your own:

- A drawing compass (for making circles) and a protractor

STEPS

Lay the tracing sheet over the page at right and trace the diagram as you follow the steps below.

1. Draw the Outer Circle (A).

2. Draw the Inner Circle (B). (Both circles use the same center point.)

The distance between the outer circle (A) and the inner circle (B) is the width of the ribbon.

3. Draw the Vertical Axis (C) all the way cross the circles, through the center point.

4. Draw the Horizontal Axis (D) perpendicular to the vertical axis, through the center point.

5. Draw diagonal lines (E and F) at 45 degree angles to (C) and (D), through the center point.

6. Draw more diagonal lines dividing in half the spaces between existing diagonal lines (G, H, I, J).

7. Number the lines clockwise around the ring.

8. Draw the first curve of the ribbon beginning on the outer circle at 1, curving down to the inner circle at 2 and back up to the outer circle at 3 (red line).

9. Draw the second curve of the ribbon parallel to the first one (blue line).

10. Rotate the tracing sheet and trace the pair of curves, now beginning at 3 and ending at 5. Continue copying the curves around the circle starting and ending at the odd numbers.

11. To create a double ribbon ring, repeat Step 9, but begin at 2 and copy the curves at even numbers.

12. Erase sections of curves to create waves or coils following the instructions on pages 72, 74 and 82.

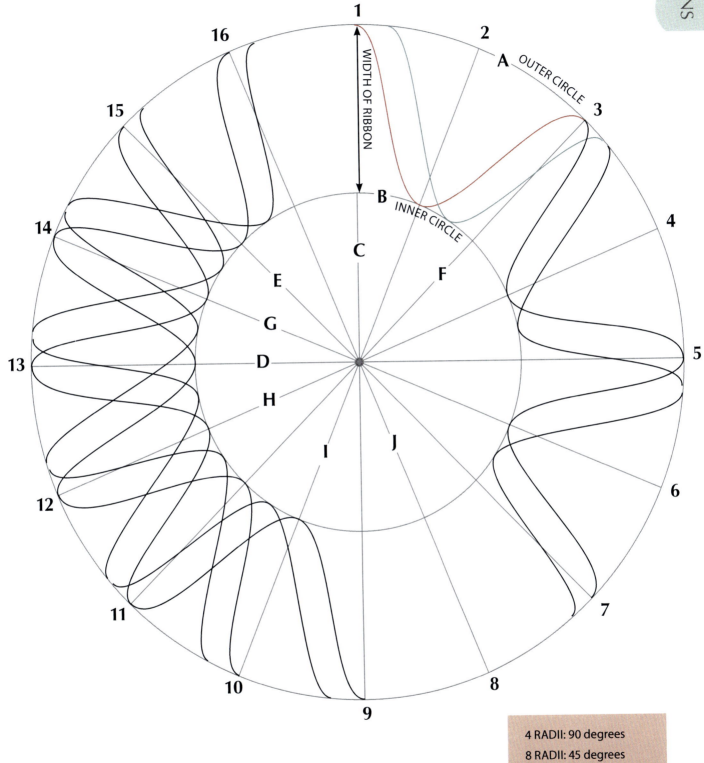

WIDTH OF RIBBON

OUTER CIRCLE

INNER CIRCLE

1
2
3
4
5
6
7
8
9
10
11
12
13
14
15
16

A
B
C
D
E
F
G
H
I
J

4 RADII: 90 degrees
8 RADII: 45 degrees
16 RADII: 22.5 degrees
32 RADII: 11.25 degrees
64 RADII: 5.625 degrees

MARRIAGE EQUALITY CELEBRATION FIREWORKS
Designed, sewn and quilted
by Karen Hostetler
48" x 48"

Coiled ribbons explode in a rainbow of colors, made even more exuberant with quilting in metallic thread and sparkling crystals. Raw edge appliqué.

CHAPTER 4

Designing & Making

Your Sideways Spiral Quilt

You've learned to draw chains, ropes and ribbons, and now you're ready to make a quilt! Sideways spirals can be used in many different ways in a quilt design. They can be the main elements or just the borders. They can be evenly sized or free-form, whimsical or elegant—whatever suits your taste.

If you're excited to start designing your own quilt, the next section will take you through the process.

If you want a design all ready to go, look at the projects beginning on page 129.

Get Creative!

Sideways Spirals can easily be adapted fit your individual style. See if some of the ideas here inspire you.

Piece charms

Foundation piecing is particularly good for this.

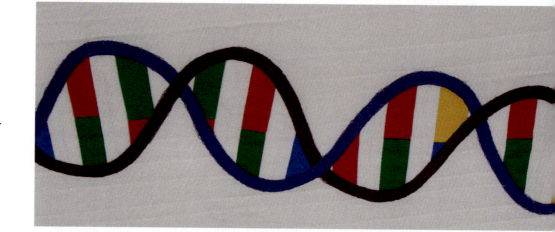

Outline

a chain, rope or ribbon and leave the fabric out altogether.

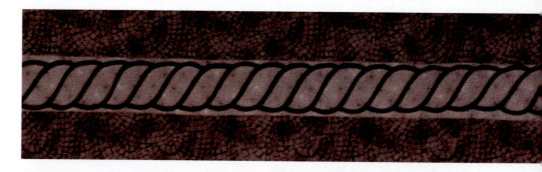

Instead of bias tape

outline chains, ropes, and ribbons with decorative trims like rickrack, ribbons, couched cording or gold braid. (For a bulky trim, you may need a couching foot on your sewing machine.) Simple satin stitching is another possibility.

Add decorative elements

Crystals, beads, buttons, found objects, etc.

Print photos on fabric

for charms. Use printable fabric sheets such as EQ Printables (see Resources, page 162).

Fussy-cut motifs from a fabric.

Do more than outline

with bias tape or trim. Add loops and twists between the charms in a chain, or add smaller-scale elements to a rope or ribbon design.

Cut windows in the charms

Instead of putting something in a charm, leave something out.

Just quilt it

Leave out the fabric altogether, and just use chains, ropes or ribbons as quilting designs (look at the image above, too).

Print, paint, appliqué, embroider or stencil lettering

on charms to spell out a special message for someone you love. (See Resources, page 162 for lettering sources.)

Using Decorative Stitches

Decorative stitching can add an elegant or whimsical detail to the outline of a rope or chain. Use a solid or a subtle texture for the bias tape so the stitching shows clearly.

Decorative stitching over the bias tape that outlines a chain or rope is an easy and fun way to add a distinctive and personal touch to your quilt. If you are not familiar with decorative stitching on your sewing machine, this is a good time to find out what stitches it might have and learn how to use them. Get out the manual or find it online and learn what your machine can do.

Older machines used cams—either insertable or built-in—to create decorative stitches. Most of today's machines are computerized, and many offer features such as these:

REVERSE OR MIRROR PATTERN – This lets you select a decorative stitch pattern and program the machine to stitch it reverse and/or mirror position.

COMBINE PATTERNS – This lets you select and program a combination of decorative stitches, including reverse and mirror pattern stitches.

Besides the decorative stitches themselves, other features you might find handy are:

AUTOMATIC LOCK STITCH – On my machine this is a button with an icon that looks like a knot. Pressed before I begin stitching, it makes three stitches in place to lock the stitches, then begins the decorative pattern. Pressed while I'm stitching, it finishes the pattern and then takes three stitches in place to lock the stitching. On some machines, the lock stitch is 3 or 4 reverse stitches. If your machine has a lock stitch button, learn how it works.

AUTOMATIC THREAD TRIMMER – This trims both top and bottom threads on the back of the fabric after you finish sewing, so thread ends are hidden. It also sets the take-up lever into its highest position so that when you begin stitching again the thread will not pull out of the needle (fantastic for foundation piecing).

AUTOMATIC TENSION – Computerized machines usually have automatic top thread tension which adjusts itself to suit the stitch pattern. However, if you find it necessary to adjust the tension manually, don't be afraid to do so. Loosening the top thread tension sometimes improves a decorative stitch.

Planning a Spiral Chain or Rope Quilt

Now you've got the idea - let's turn it into a quilt! Gather your tools: In addition to a sewing machine, iron and basic sewing tools, here is what you will need. I've included a few different materials for making bias tape, depending on the method you choose (see pages 96-100).

WHAT YOU'LL NEED FOR DRAFTING

- Pencil and paper for drafting the pattern
- Straight ruler, flexible curve ruler and/or French curve template (page 18)
- Measuring tape (for measuring curved lines around charms and rope sections)

WHAT YOU'LL NEED FOR SEWING

- Rotary cutter, mat and 24˝ ruler
- Paper-backed fusible web (such as Wonder Under or Steam-a-Seam)
- Pressing sheet and/or scratch paper (to protect iron and ironing board while fusing)
- Bias tape makers (see page 98)
- Options for bias tape:
  Water-soluble thread
  Fusible thread
  Silk or polyester thread for topstitching
  Fabric glue
- Stiletto or bamboo skewer (helps with sewing bias tape around curves)
- Invisible polyester thread (don't get nylon— it may melt when ironed)

DRAFTING A PATTERN

As you learned in the exercises earlier in the book, spiral chains and ropes are simple to draw. Start with a small sketch, then draft it full size on any paper— art pad, freezer paper, or whatever you have handy. You can use the graph technique on page 138 in the *Flying Free* project to enlarge a small drawing to full size. Use a flexible curve ruler and/or a French curve template to smooth curved lines.

Once the design is drafted full size, there are a few important things to do:

1. Number charms in a chain so you'll know in what order to put them together (A). Rope sections need to be numbered if they are different shapes and/or sizes.

2. Mark charms if necessary to indicate which side is up or down, right or left. (Sometimes just the direction of the writing will be enough.) For ropes, mark a line down the center and dots where each rope section touches the next one (B).

3. Make a copy of the design for reference. It can be any size you want—even just a photograph on your phone—as long as you can read the markings on it.

Once you have labeled and copied your design, you can cut up the full-size copy for templates.

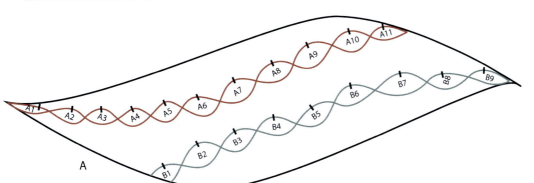

A

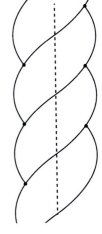

B

Choosing Fabrics for Chains and Ropes

My favorite part of making any quilt! Choose fabrics that are different enough in proportion and value to be seen against each other. Use contrasting colors, values and pattern sizes to separate and define the different elements of your design.

Backgrounds

A dense, medium-sized print is best. Smaller prints and solids will work as well. Don't use large, busy prints: they hide the charms or rope sections and the bias tape over them (compare the pictures below).

Charms in a Chain

The goal here is to make the charms pop off the background fabric. If the background fabric is busy, for the charms use a solid color, or a solid color behind any letters or other figures. With a plain background fabric the charms can be busy.

Rope Sections

Alternate two colors or values to give the rope a clear twist. Monochrome prints and textures work best.

Bias Tape

Solids or tiny monochrome prints are best. Use solids if you plan to do decorative stitching over the bias tape. In chains, get the maximum spiral effect by using two different colors for the outline. They should be the same value, and they should both contrast clearly with the background and the charms. In ropes, use the same color bias tape throughout.

Compare the difference between a busy background and a quieter one. On the busy background fabric, the flowers are almost as large (and the same colors) as the rope sections so the rope gets lost. The more solid background highlights the rope.

Fabric choices: Solids, textures, tiny prints and small stripes work best for bias tape. If you plan to put decorative stitching over it, use a solid or subtle texture.

CALCULATING YARDAGE

Background, Backing & Batting

1. Measure the height (H) by the width (W) of the finished quilt.

2. (H) x (W) = square inches.

3. Divide square inches by 1440 = yardage.

4. Add some extra for squaring up, seam allowances, etc.

Charms & Rope Sections

1. Measure the height (HC) and width (WC) of the charm or rope sections.

2. Count the charms or rope sections (#).

3. Multiply (HC) x (WC) x (#) = square inches.

4. Divide square inches by 1440 = yardage.

5. If you're fussy-cutting motifs, count the number of motifs you need in the fabric.

Bias Tape for Charms

1. Measure around a charm for its circumference (C). (If they aren't all the same size, measure a large one.)

2. Count the charms (#).

3. Decide on the finished width of the bias tape and multiply it by 2 (BT).

4. Multiply (C) x (#) x (BT) = square inches.

5. Divide square inches by 1440 = base yardage.

6. Then, since you're cutting on the bias and will lose some yardage to the corners, increase the yardage by 50% (multiply base yardage by 1.5).

Bias Tape for Ropes

1. Measure the length of the curve between two rope sections (L) (red line in diagram at right).

2. Decide on the finished width of the bias tape, then multiply it by 2 (BT)

3. (L) x (#) x (BT) = square inches.

4. Divide square inches by 1440 = base yardage.

5. Then, since you're cutting on the bias and will lose some yardage to the corners, increase the yardage by 50% (multiply base yardage by 1.5).

Binding

1. Measure Left Side (L) + Right Side (R) + Top (T) + Bottom (B) of quilt.

2. (L) + (R) + (T) + (B) = linear inches needed.

3. Multiply linear inches x 3 = square inches. (Based on 42″-44″ width, this allows for a 2½″ binding strip, plus room for squaring up fabric, diagonal seams for joining, and folding the binding at corners).

4. Divide square inches by 1440 = base yardage. Use this amount if you are cutting binding on grain.

5. If you're cutting on the bias you will lose some yardage to the corners, so increase the yardage by 50% (multiply base yardage by 1.5).

Pre-wash and iron all fabrics. I have found that fusing works better when any sizing left from the manufacturing process has been washed away. For the same reason, avoid using starch.

Making Bias Tape

Bias tape is the key "ingredient" in spiral chains and ropes. It easy and fun to make with just a few simple tools. Here are several methods: some use an iron, and some make bias tape at the sewing machine.

WHAT YOU'LL NEED

- Fabric: Solids, textures, tiny prints and small stripes work best (see page 92)
- Rotary cutter, ruler and mat
- Bias tape maker

For ironed methods:
- An Iron

For ironed Method #2
- Fusible tape for Clover bias tape maker

For sewing machine methods:
- A sewing machine that will stitch a zigzag (or even better, a 3-stitch zigzag)
- A foot with a cross bar and raised toe (*not* an open toe foot)

For Sewing Machine Method #1
- Water soluble thread and regular thread

For Sewing Machine Method #2:
- Water soluble thread and fusible thread

For Sewing Machine Method #3:
- Top-stitching thread (I like Superior's Kimono Silk) and lightweight bobbin thread such as Superior's Bottom Line

For Sewing Machine Method #4:
- Bias bars (also called loop pressing bars)
- Zipper foot (see photo on page 100)

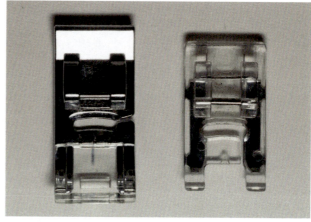

Two examples of sewing machine feet to use for making bias tape. Notice the bar across the front.

Vanish Water-soluble thread, Kimono Silk thread and Charlotte's Web Fusible Thread from Superior Threads (see Resources, page 162).

Bias tape makers. From left: Clover ¼″, ⅜″ and ½″ with a channel for fusible web tape. Far right: ½″ without channel for fusible web.

Bias tape makers come in a variety of sizes from ¼″ up to 2″. The sizes I use most are ¼″ (6mm), ⅜″ (9mm) and ½″ (12mm) . I prefer the style with a channel that holds a narrow tape of paper-backed fusible web—it can be used with or without the fusible tape.

PREPARE FABRIC STRIPS

1. Cut bias strips of fabric twice the width of the finished bias tape. (Cut 1" wider for Sewing Machine Method #4.)

2. Join strips together with diagonal seams. Press seams open and trim "ears" (A). Cut the leading end of the strip diagonally.

FOR THIS SIZE BIAS TAPE	CUT THIS WIDTH BIAS STRIP
¼"	½"
⅜"	¾"
½"	1"

A

B

Ironed Method #1

INSERT the fabric strip face up into the wide end of the bias tape maker. Use a pin to advance the fabric. Pull a 2" tail out of the tip (B). Anchor the tail of the bias strip to your ironing board with a pin. The folded side of the bias tape can be either up or down.

IRON: Place the tip of the iron right at the tip of the bias tape maker, so the fabric does not have a chance to unfold when it passes from the tool to the iron (C). Hold the bias tape maker by the handle and slowly pull it along the bias strip away from the pin, keeping the iron at its tip as you go. Re-anchor with the pin and continue down the strip as necessary.

POSITION: Use fabric glue or zigzag stitch with water-soluble thread for a temporary bond. Then, stitch permanently using visible or invisible thread along the edges. Add decorative stitching over the bias tape if you wish. When the bias tape is secure, rinse away water-soluble thread.

Ironed Method 2: Fusible tape

Everything about this method is the same as Method 1, except:
INSERT the fusible web strip into the channel of the bias tape maker and under the bar at the tip with the fusible side down. Insert the fabric strip into the bias tape maker with the folded side of the bias tape up and the fusible tape on top of the fold. Anchor fusible tape and fabric with a pin.

IRON: Press slowly so the fusible web has time to fuse to the back of the bias tape (D). Take care not to stretch the bias tape; if the fabric stretches, when it contracts again a bridge will form in the fusible tape.

POSITION: Fuse this bias tape temporarily on your quilt with an iron. Handle the work with care until the bias tape is stitched securely into place with invisible thread and/or decorative stitching.

TIP

Take care to keep seams pressed open as they enter the back of the bias tape maker. Slow down and gently ease them through the tip to avoid stretching.

C

D

RESULT: Top, front of the folded bias tape. Bottom, fusible web tape on back of bias tape (paper still on).

SEWING MACHINE METHODS

Sewing your bias tape creates a secure fold and you don't have to bother with an iron. Put the bias tape maker right in front of the sewing machine foot, then zigzag to hold the folds in place.

Set-up and instructions for Sewing Machine Methods #1-3

1. Put a raised-toe, crossbar foot on the sewing machine (page 96).

2. Set the machine for a 3-stitch zigzag (A) or decorative stitch. Make sure you're using a throat plate for zigzag. Set the stitch width a little less than the finished width of the bias tape. (If you don't have 3-stitch zigzag, use a regular zigzag.)

A

3. Loosen the top tension a bit (B). The top thread should loop underneath to the bottom just a bit, so that any bobbin thread left underneath the bias tape will not be visible.

4. Use top and bobbin threads indicated in each method.

5. Prepare fabric strips as shown on page 97.

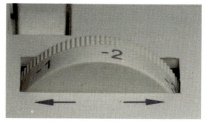

B

6. Insert the bias strip into the bias tape maker and pull a 2-3″ tail out. Pin the tail folded.

7. Put the tail under the sewing machine foot with the folded side down. Let about 1″ of fabric extend behind the foot.

8. Lower the foot.

9. Place the tip of the bias tape maker as far under the raised toe as it fits. Hold it centered against the foot as you sew.

> **TIP**
>
> With Method #1 or #2 you can stitch bias tape directly onto the background fabric, or even onto a layered quilt sandwich.

10. Sew, allowing the feed dogs to advance the bias tape. You may need to grasp the tape behind the foot and gently help advance it. Don't worry if it stretches a bit—the zigzag stitch will allow it to contract back to its normal width.

Sewing Machine Method #1: Water-Soluble Thread

TOP THREAD: Water-soluble thread.

BOBBIN THREAD: Water-soluble thread or any other thread. (This is a good place to use that old mystery thread you inherited from your grandmother!)

STITCH with a 3-stitch zigzag.

POSITION: Use fabric glue or stitch again with water-soluble thread for a temporary bond. Then, stitch permanently using visible or invisible thread along the edges. Add decorative stitching over the bias tape if you wish. When the bias tape is secure, rinse away water-soluble thread.

Top thread: Vanish Lite water-soluble thread from Superior Threads (see Resources, page 162). Bobbin thread: Anything, even old mystery thread.

RESULT: Top, the front of the bias tape stitched with water-soluble thread. Below, the back of the bias tape stitched with regular thread.

Sewing Machine Method #2: Fusible Thread

TOP THREAD: Water-soluble thread.

BOBBIN THREAD: Fusible thread.

STITCH with a 3-stitch zigzag.

POSITION: Iron bias tape into place following the manufacturer's instructions. Then, stitch permanently using visible or invisible thread along the edges. Add decorative stitching over the bias tape if you wish. When the bias tape is secure, rinse away water-soluble thread.

Top thread: Vanish Lite Water-soluble Thread. Bobbin thread: Charlotte's Web Fusible Thread (see Resources, page 162).

RESULT: Top, the front of the bias tape stitched with water-soluble thread. Below, the back of the bias tape stitched with fusible thread.

Sewing Machine Method #3: Decorative Stitching

TOP THREAD Fine topstitching thread (silk or glossy polyester is nice).

BOBBIN THREAD Lightweight bobbin thread such as Bottom Line.

STITCH with a decorative stitch (see page 92).

POSITION Use fabric glue or stitch over the decorative stitching with water-soluble thread for a temporary bond. Then, stitch permanently with visible or invisible thread along the edges. When the bias tape is secure, rinse away water-soluble thread.

Kimono Silk Thread from Superior is one of my favorite threads for topstitching as well as fine quilting (see Resources, page 162).

RESULT: Top, the front of the bias tape stitched with a decorative stitch in silk thread. Below, the back of the bias tape stitched with Bottom Line. Loosening the top tension allowed the top thread to come to the back. Newer machines may make this adjustment automatically. Test the tension before sewing.

Sewing Machine Method #4: Bias Bars

TOP & BOBBIN THREADS Any regular sewing thread; may be old thread.

STITCH with a straight stitch.

1. Cut fabric strips extra wide so they catch on the feed dogs.

2. Wrap fabric strips right-side out around a bias bar (also called a loop pressing bar). They should be snug but not tight or stretched.

3. Use a zipper foot and move the needle to the left in order to stitch as closely to the bar as possible without hitting it.

4. After sewing, trim seam allowance to ⅛″, turn the seam allowance to the center of the bar and press.

POSITION With the seam hidden underneath, use fabric glue or stitch in place with water-soluble thread for a temporary bond. Then, stitch permanently using visible or invisible thread along the edges. Add decorative stitching over the bias tape if you wish. When the bias tape is secure, rinse away water-soluble thread.

Assembling a Spiral Chain

This is fun, though at moments all the bias tape might make you feel as though you've gotten tangled in an oversized plate of spaghetti!

MAKE THE CHARMS

1. Trace the charm templates onto the front of the charm fabric.

2. Number them and mark left and right sides, if necessary.

3. Copy any alignment marks, keeping them within ¼″ of the edge so they will be covered with bias tape.

4. Iron fusible web onto the back. Cut out the charms along the lines.

Here's a quirky little thing you need to watch out for: If the charms are NOT symmetrical and you trace the charms onto the paper side of the fusible web rather than the front of the fabric, you need to trace the charm in REVERSE position onto the paper of the fusible web. This way, the charm will turn out in original position when you cut out the charm and position it face up on the background.

MAKE THE BIAS TAPE

Prepare bias tape using one of the methods on pages 96-100.

PREPARE THE BACKGROUND

1. Cut and/or sew the background fabric to the desired size.

2. If necessary, mark the placement of the charms. If you need to position a template, follow the instructions for preparing the background in the *Flying Free* project (page 138).

PLACE THE CHARMS

1. Arrange the charms on the background fabric so they touch at the tips but do not overlap. If you wish, adjust shapes at tight curves to make an easier connection and a smoother curve for the bias tape.

2. Remove the paper from the back of each charm and fuse it into place according to the manufacturer's instructions. Cover the charm with paper or a pressing sheet to prevent any fusible web from getting on the iron.

TIP

A removable fabric marker is good for labeling charms and marking background placement, but don't iron over it. Some markers (such as the blue water-soluble ones) can be set with heat and others (such as Frixion markers) disappear with heat.

If you iron over a Frixion marker, try putting the fabric in the freezer for a little while: the cold makes the wax-based ink reappear.

TIP

To easily remove the paper backing, score it with the tip of a straight pin.

BUILD THE CHAIN

1. Starting at the edge of the background, lay Color #1 bias tape or decorative trim (black in diagram below) around the left side of Charm #1/2 and around the right side of the Charm #1. Don't stretch the bias tape; instead, ease and flatten it on the inside edge of the curve. Stitch, glue or fuse (according to whichever bias tape method you used) up to 1″ before the end of Charm #1.

2. Starting at the edge of the background, lay Color #2 bias tape or decorative trim (light blue in diagram below) around the right side of Charm #1/2, around the left side of Charm #1 and around the right side of Charm #2. Stitch, glue or fuse up to 1″ before the end of Charm #2.

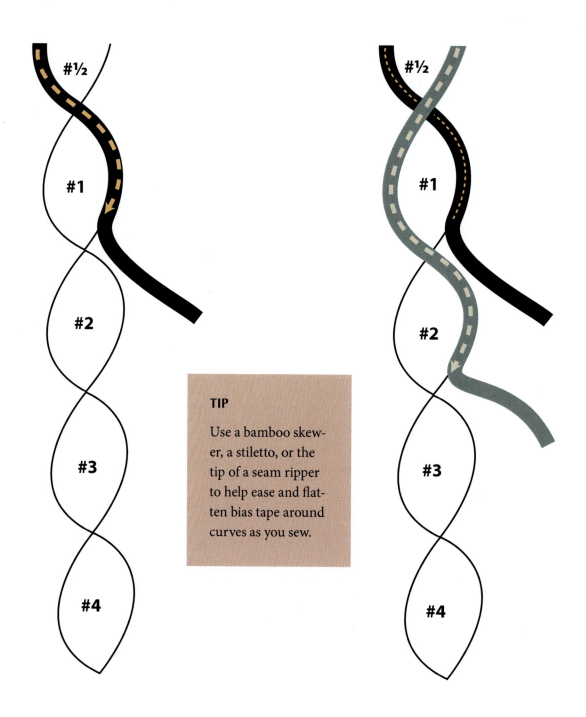

TIP

Use a bamboo skewer, a stiletto, or the tip of a seam ripper to help ease and flatten bias tape around curves as you sew.

3. Starting at the end of the stitching on Charm #1 lay Color #1 bias tape along the left side of Charm #2 and around the right side of Charm #3. Stitch or glue up to 1″ before the end of Charm #3.

4. Starting at the end of the stitching on Charm #2 lay Color #2 bias tape along the left side of Charm #3 and around the right side of Charm #4. Stitch or glue up to 1″ before the end of Charm #4.

Continue to glue, stitch or fuse the bias strips around the charms, repeating Steps 3 and 4. The bias strips will twist over and under into a spiral.

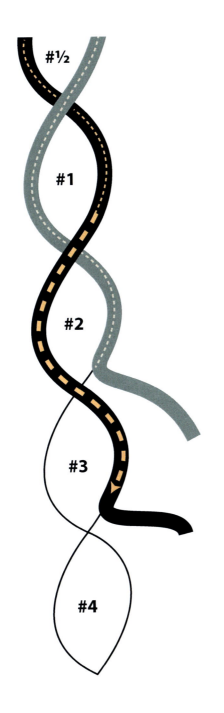

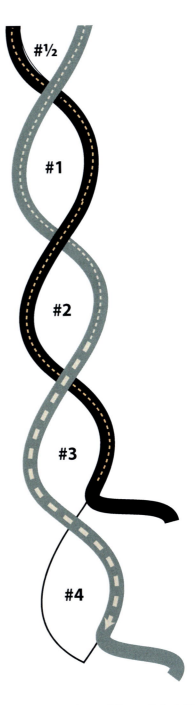

Assembling a Rope

The key to assembling a rope is leaving an unattached section of bias tape so you can hide the end of the next bias tape under it.

PREPARE THE ROPE SECTIONS

1. So that the rope will twist in the direction that you drew it, make a REVERSE copy of the rope section template(s). Include numbers and markings.

2. Trace the reverse rope template onto the paper of the fusible web for as many rope sections as you'll need. Include all numbers and markings.

3. Iron the fusible web to the backs of the rope fabrics.

4. Cut out the rope sections. Do not remove the paper.

PREPARE THE BACKGROUND

1. Cut and/or sew background to the desired size.

2. On the front of the background fabric, mark the center line of the rope. If you need to copy from a template, see Preparing the Background in the *Flying Free* project (page 138.)

PREPARE THE BIAS TAPE

Use one of the methods on pages 96–100.

FUSE ROPE SECTIONS ONTO THE BACKGROUND

1. Arrange rope sections on the background, alternating colors. Align the center line on each rope section with the center line on the background fabric. (Finger-press the rope sections along the center line so you can see it.) The edges of the sections should touch but not overlap.

2. Remove the paper from the rope sections and fuse them into place.

OUTLINE THE ROPE WITH BIAS TAPE

BIAS STRIP #1 (YELLOW DASHED LINE): Starting at A, sew, glue or fuse a strip of bias tape over the edge of the rope section. Stop at B and skip to C, leaving about 1″ unattached. (This is where you'll tuck the end of the next strip under.) End at D. (Note: There may be partial sections at the edge of the background. If so, start at the partial sections (a1 then a2) and work up the rope to the whole sections.)

BIAS STRIP #2 (RED DASHED LINE): Start a new bias strip at E, and sew, glue or fuse to F. Stop and skip to G, leaving about 1″ unattached between F and G. At G, resume sewing, gluing or fusing. Tuck end of this bias strip under Bias Strip #1 between B and C. Finish at H. Continue working up the rope, outlining each section in the same order.

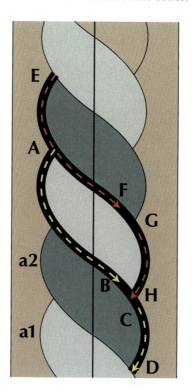

Add Decorative Stitching

If you made bias tape using Sewing Machine Method #3 (page 100) you already added decorative stitching to the bias tape. If you didn't do it then, you can add it now, before you begin quilting.

1. Stitch along each separate length of bias tape (the order doesn't matter).

2. Stop and start the decorative stitch each time it is crossed by another bias tape. Use a lock stitch at the beginning and end of each run so threads don't work loose.

See page 92 for more about decorative stitching.

Decorative stitching on a chain

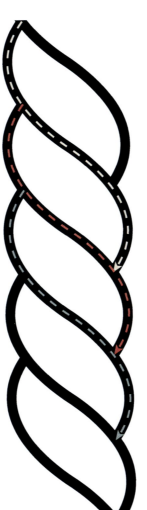

Decorative stitching on a rope

Decorative stitching on a twist

Quilting Spiral Chains and Ropes

Once you have the bias tape temporarily fixed into place on a rope or chain, decide whether the permanent stitching will be visible or invisible. When you are ready to quilt, the order of the steps differs, depending on whether you use a home machine or a longarm machine. If you use a home machine, the stitching that holds the bias tape in place can also be the first step of the quilting.

INVISIBLE STITCHING

Use invisible stitching along the edges of the bias tape if you don't want the stitching to be seen, and if you do decorative stitching along its center.

Thread the sewing machine with invisible polyester thread in the top and bobbin. (Don't use nylon thread, as it can become brittle and yellow after a few years. It may also melt if you iron it.) Set the machine for a narrow zigzag stitch—.1 width, 2.0 length. One side of the zigzag should catch just a few threads of the bias tape fabric. The other side of the zigzag should stitch just outside the edge of the bias tape. Carefully stitch along all edges of the bias tape. Use the stitching order on the next page to stitch continuously.

VISIBLE STITCHING

Visible stitching on the bias tape edges can be a simple straight stitch or decorative edging stitch, such as a buttonhole stitch. The thread color can match or contrast with the bias tape. Stitch along all edges of the bias tape, working in the order shown on the next page.

A straight stitch should fall just inside the edge of the bias tape. With an edging stitch, the outside of the stitch should fall just outside the edge of the bias tape. Stop stitching and lock-stitch or tie off the thread whenever one bias tape passes under the other. This will preserve the twisting effect of the spiral.

Invisible stitching

Straight-stitch edge stitching

OUTLINING A CHAIN OR ROPE

To outline a spiral chain or rope with invisible stitching, outline stitching or quilting, stitch in this order. Trace the diagrams with your finger to get the pattern before you begin stitching.

First line of stitching (Blue line, both diagrams)

Stitch along one outside edge all the way along the chain or rope (A - B - C).

Second line of stitching (Red line, both diagrams)

1. On the other side of the chain or rope, stitch up to a crossover (1).

2. Stitch along the outside edge to the next crossover (2).

3. Turn and stitch into the center of the charm or rope section (3).

4. Stitch along the inside edge up to the previous crossover (4).

5. Stitch over the bias tape toward the outside of the chain or rope section, then return over the same line of stitching back to the inside (5).

6. Stitch along the other inside edge of the charm or rope section back to where you turned inside (6).

7. Turn toward the outside of the chain or rope and stitch over the entry stitches to exit (7).

8. Repeat from Step 1 for each charm or rope section.

QUILTING ON A HOME MACHINE

Sandwich the quilt first, then stitch along the edges of the bias tape. The edge stitching becomes the first lines of quilting. Fill in the background as you wish.

QUILTING ON A LONG ARM MACHINE

Since a longarm machine doesn't do zigzag or decorative stitches, stitch down the edges of the bias tape on your home machine before you sandwich the quilt. Then, sandwich the top, batting and backing. Outline the spiral chain or rope, then fill in the background as you wish. (This method can also be used on a home machine.)

After quilting, rinse or wash the quilt to remove any water-soluble thread or glue.

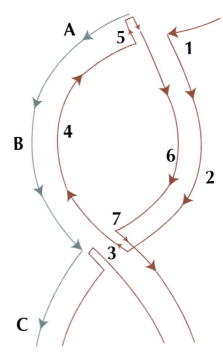

Stitching order to outline a chain

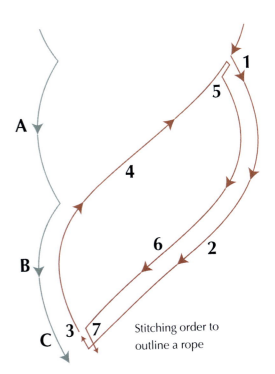

Stitching order to outline a rope

Planning a Ribbon Quilt

Ribbons can be constructed either with appliqué or piecing. Begin by choosing the construction method you'll use. (You'll find more information about each method on page 110.) Then, go to pages 112-127 for specific instructions on building waves, coils and double ribbons.

APPLIQUÉ-IN-A-TRACK

Appliqué-in-a-track is my preferred method for assembling a ribbon. The pieces of the ribbon are appliquéd onto background fabric that is cut the size and shape of the track (either straight or curved), with added seam allowances on the sides. The ribbon pieces extend into the seam allowance (A). When the ribbon is complete, sew the track into the larger quilt (B). Either turned-edge or raw-edge appliqué can be used.

Appliqué-in-a-track has several advantages. One, it minimizes the amount of background fabric you have to handle for the appliqué. More importantly from a design standpoint, if you're using a trim or satin stitch over a raw edge, the track seam prevents the edge treatment from appearing where the ribbon bends, exactly the way a real ribbon would look. So appliqué-in-a-track produces more realistic-looking ribbons.

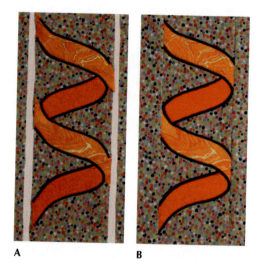

A   B

APPLIQUÉ

Of course you can appliqué a ribbon without the track, using either turned-edge appliqué (C) or raw-edge appliqué (D). If you have overlapping ribbons this may be the best approach, so that one track does not interrupt another. However, for raw-edge appliqué with satin-stitching or trim along the edges, this is my least favorite method because it places an outline at the bend where a real ribbon would not have one (D). In this case, use an outline thread that matches the fabric.

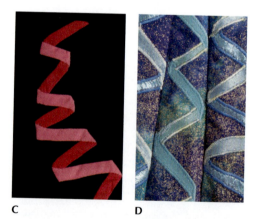

C   D

PIECING

Piecing a ribbon also involves building the ribbon in a track then sewing it into the larger quilt. As with appliqué-in-a-track, the track creates the bend to create a realistic-looking ribbon.

Piecing can be done on a sewing machine or by hand. Although you are sewing curves, it is easier than you might think. Sewing order is critical here: follow the numbering diagrams on the following pages exactly to minimize curves and avoid unnecessary "Y" seams. Accurate marking and pinning are key to getting everything to fit properly so carefully follow the construction techniques on page 111.

Preparing to Sew

When your design is ready to turn into a quilt, follow these steps to prepare templates, then gather your tools and get started!

WHAT YOU'LL NEED FOR DRAFTING

- Paper for drafting the pattern
- Pencil and eraser
- Straight ruler
- Flexible curve ruler and/or French curve template
- Scissors for paper

WHAT YOU'LL NEED FOR SEWING

- Sewing machine, iron & basic sewing tools
- Rotary cutter, mat and 24″ ruler
- Removable fabric marker
- Permanent double-sided tape (I prefer Scotch brand in the yellow and red box)

For raw-edge appliqué:

- Fabric glue stick, or
- Paper-backed fusible web (such as Wonder Under)
- Pressing sheet (to protect iron and ironing board while fusing)
- Thread for satin-stitching edges

For turned-edge appliqué:

- Freezer paper, or
- Wash-away appliqué sheets
- Edge-turning tools, if you use them

DRAFTING A PATTERN

1. Draft the design full-size on paper. (See the enlarging technique in the *Flying Free* project, page 138.)

2. Number ribbon sections in the order they'll be assembled (see instructions for each type of ribbon on pages 112-127).

3. Mark where ribbon pieces pass under other ribbon pieces.

4. Place alignment marks where pieces join.

5. Make a copy of the design for reference. It can be any size—even just a photograph on your phone—as long as you can read the markings on it.

6. If you're appliquéing, trace the ribbon onto the front of the background fabric with a removable fabric marker. You may need to darken the lines of the template with a black marker and/or put the template and fabric on a light box or window in order to see the lines through the fabric.

7. Cut up the full-size drawing for templates.

8. Use the templates to cut the pieces of fabric (see Cutting Fabric, page 110). Use double-sided tape to adhere templates to the fabric.

Choosing Fabrics for Ribbons

Ribbons create the illusion of three dimensions on a two-dimensional surface. Value and pattern are essential in creating the effect.

VALUE

Choose two fabrics in different values for a ribbon. Remember that light values come forward and dark values fall back, so place the lighter fabric where the ribbon passes over, and the darker fabric where the ribbon passes under. Two values of the same color are the best choice, but it is possible to use two different colors—just make sure that they are similar enough so that they appear to be part of the same ribbon.

Look through the many examples in the gallery of ribbon quilts to see how light and dark values enhance the dimensionality of the ribbons.

Use a light value and a dark value of the same color to create the three-dimensional effect of a twisting ribbon.

If you are doing a double ribbon design, the two ribbons should be different colors. For each ribbon, use a light value and a dark value of the same color.

SOLIDS OR PATTERNS?

SOLIDS: Solid fabrics (which include tiny monochrome prints and textures that read as solid) allow the eye to travel along the line of the ribbon without distraction. If you are doing a design with multiple ribbons, solids are likely the best choice, since the eye already must separate different colors to follow the lines of different ribbons; introducing pattern could confuse the design.

PATTERNS: If the fabric has a pattern, the best choices are small-scale prints. Colors should be spread uniformly throughout the pattern so the ribbon sections are all colored the same.

If one fabric in a ribbon is a print, use a solid for the other, so the patterns don't mush together, unless the values of the colors separate them strongly enough.

A print in a background fabric should be much smaller than the ribbon sections, otherwise the ribbon sections will get lost in the background pattern.

The solids help hold the pattern. The colors in the patterns are uniformly distributed so all the ribbon sections would be colored the same, providing visual continuity.

These patterns work together because the designs are similar while the values separate them.

CALCULATING YARDAGE

Background, Backing & Batting

1. Measure the height (H) by the width (W) of the finished quilt.

2. (H) x (W) = square inches.

3. Divide square inches by 1440 = yardage.

4. Add some extra for squaring up, seam allowances, etc.

Ribbon Sections & Fusible Web

1. Measure the height (H) and width (W) of the largest ribbon section, including any seam allowances.

2. Count the ribbon sections (#).

3. Multiply (H) x (W) x (#) = square inches.

4. Divide square inches by 1440 = yardage.

5. Add some extra for squaring up, seam allowances, etc.

Trim for Edges of Ribbons

1. Measure one side of one full ribbon section. Multiply by 2. This is the amount you'll need for both sides of one full section (RS).

2. Count the number of ribbon sections (#).

3. (RS) x (#) = linear inches of trim needed.

4. Divide by 36 for yards.

Binding

1. Measure Left Side (L) + Right Side (R) + Top (T) + Bottom (B) of quilt.

2. (L) + (R) + (T) + (B) = linear inches needed.

3. Multiply linear inches x 3 = square inches. (Based on 42″-44″ width, this allows for a 2½″ binding strip, plus room for squaring up fabric, diagonal seams for joining, and folding the binding at corners).

4. Divide square inches by 1440 = base yardage. Use this amount if you are cutting binding on grain.

5. If you're cutting on the bias you will lose some yardage to the corners, so increase the yardage by 50% (multiply base yardage by 1.5).

Pre-wash and iron all fabrics. I have found that fusing works better when any sizing left from the manufacturing process has been washed away. For the same reason, avoid using starch.

Color- or value-graduated fabrics give you the opportunity to enhance dimensionality in your ribbons even more than just using a light and a dark fabric. Place darker values inside the bend of the ribbon and lighter values on the outside of the bend. Using gradations would take some planning and fussy-cutting, but the results could be spectacular.

Construction Techniques for Ribbons

Here are some important techniques for assembling ribbons. Use the techniques that correspond to the construction method you choose.

CUTTING FABRIC

The method of construction you choose determines whether or not seam allowances need to be added around the ribbon templates:

Appliqué-in-a-Track (AIAT)

RIBBON SECTIONS: Place templates face up on front of fabric. Cut at edge of templates along sides but leave extensions at ends so they reach to the side of the track. (This allows them to be caught in the track.) Also leave extensions at ends where ribbon sections lie under other ribbon sections. (This lets you overlap pieces, leaving only one raw edge to cover with stitching or trim).

BACKGROUND: Full size and shape of the track, plus ¼″ seam allowance on all sides.

Turned-edge appliqué (TEA)

RIBBON SECTIONS: Place templates face up on front of fabric or face down on back of fabric. Add ¼″ seam allowance on all sides.

BACKGROUND: Solid piece of fabric as fits the overall quilt design.

Raw-edge appliqué (without a track) (REA)

RIBBON SECTIONS: Place templates face up on front of fabric. Add seam allowance only at ends where ribbon sections overlap.

BACKGROUND: Solid piece of fabric as fits the overall quilt design.

Piecing

RIBBON AND BACKGROUND: Place templates face down on back of fabric. Mark outline of template. Add approximate ¼″ seam allowance on all sides.

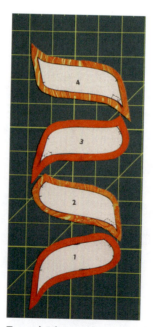

Appliqué-in-a-Track
Seam allowances at track edges and overlaps

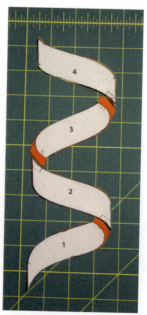

Turned-Edge Appliqué
Seam allowance on all sides

Raw-Edge Appliqué (without a track)
Seam allowance at overlaps only

Piecing
Seam allowance on all sides

PIECING RIBBONS

PINNING: Pin precisely on the alignment marks and seam lines both front and back (A, B). Use a lot of pins, placed close together (particularly on curves0 so that there is no chance the two fabrics can slip out of alignment. Pin and sew on the side where the fabric bends back from the curve (C). It's okay to stop the machine every couple of stitches with the needle down, lift the presser foot and rotate the fabric a bit to stay on the line of the curve.

STITCHING BY MACHINE: Stitch along the seam line until the point of the pin is two stitch-lengths in front of the needle (D). Grasp the head of the pin in your right hand and hold it so it cannot advance with the fabric. Stitch slowly without letting the pin move forward—the feed dogs on the machine are pulling the fabric off the pin. The fabric stays pinned until just before it goes under the needle so it never has a chance to slip out of alignment. (You can see a short video of this technique on my YouTube channel. Just search for "Good to the last stitch pinning.")

STITCHING BY HAND: Check both sides of the fabric each time you take a stitch to make sure that the needle stays on the marked seam line on both sides.

SEAM ALLOWANCES: Press seam allowances toward the ribbon whenever possible. Don't press seams open, because that creates a line where there is no fabric.

Sometimes, near the side of the track, seam allowances must be clipped and pressed outward in order to have a seam allowance at the edge (E).

When hand-piecing, never stitch down a seam allowance that you are crossing. Stitch under or through it, leaving the seam allowance to move freely from side to side. When it's time to press, you can decide which way you want the seam allowance to fall.

A

B

C

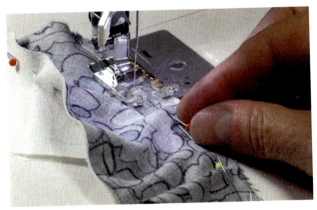

D

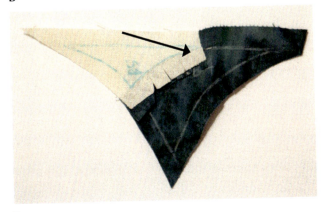

E

Assembling a Wave

Appliqué or Appliqué-in-a-Track

Think of a wave as a folded stack of ribbon and construct it from the bottom layer up. Notice in the photograph below that the ribbon has a "front" edge (the solid line) and a "back" edge (the dashed line). Add satin-stitching or trim on the back edges as you build, then on the front edge at the end.

> This practice template can be found in the online library. See page 3 for address and password.

> The photos here show appliqué-in-a-track (AIAT) using raw-edge appliqué (REA) in order to demonstrate the order of adding edge-stitching or trim. The assembly order for the ribbon is the same for either raw-edge or turned-edge appliqué (TEA), whether or not you are using a track. Raw-edge appliqué can be either fused or glued.

1. Mark the template.

Color the ribbon to show the front side (light) and back side (dark).

Number the ribbon sections from the bottom layer up.

On the ribbon, place alignment marks at edges of ribbon where sections overlap (X's).

AIAT: Add ¼″ seam allowance outside the track on both sides (Y's). Where the ribbon meets the track lines, mark the point where each curve touches the line (Z's).

2. Cut the ribbon and background fabrics. Follow the instructions on page 112 for the appliqué method you are using. Place templates face up on the front of the fabric.

3. Mark the position of the ribbon pieces on the background fabric with a removable fabric marker.

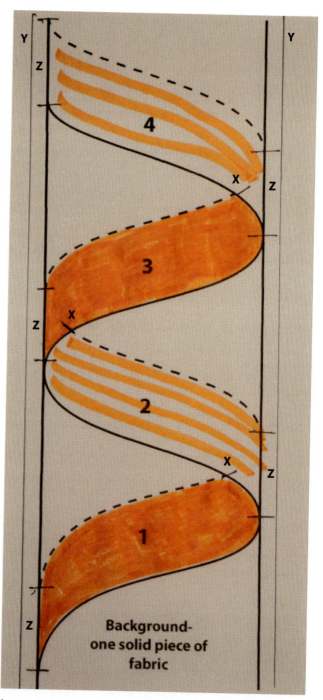

1

4. Begin at whichever end of the wave has the lowest layer. Appliqué piece 1.

TEA: Leave unsewn the end that will lie under piece 2 (A).

AIAT: Outer end of ribbon extends to edge of track (B).

4A. REA: Satin stitch or trim along back edge of piece 1 (see Note 1).

5. Appliqué piece 2 over piece 1.

TEA: Leave unsewn the end that lies under the next ribbon section (A).

AIAT: Outer end of ribbon extends to edge of track (B).

5A. REA: Satin stitch or trim along back edge of piece (see Note 1).

6. Repeat Step 5 for each ribbon section to the end of the ribbon.

AIAT: Last piece: both ends of ribbon extend to edge of track (A, B).

7. AIAT: Sew the track into the surrounding background of the quilt.

8. REA: Satin stitch along the front edge of the ribbon (see Note 2).

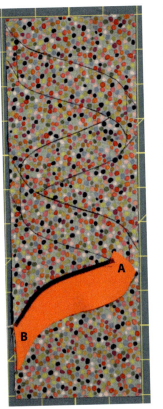

4 & 4A

5 & 5A

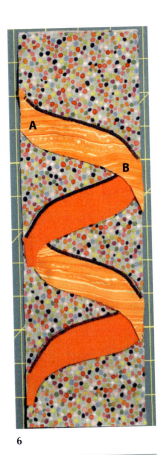

6

7

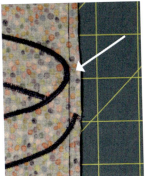

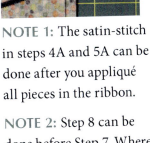

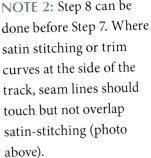

8

NOTE 1: The satin-stitch in steps 4A and 5A can be done after you appliqué all pieces in the ribbon.

NOTE 2: Step 8 can be done before Step 7. Where satin stitching or trim curves at the side of the track, seam lines should touch but not overlap satin-stitching (photo above).

Piecing a Wave

Sewing pieces together in the right order is essential when piecing a wave. Look at the photograph below and notice that the ribbon has a "front" edge (the solid line) and a "back" edge (the dashed line). Sew pieces together in pairs along the "back" edge, then join the units.

> This practice template can be found in the online library. See page 3 for address and password.

1. Mark the template

Color the ribbon to show the front side (light color, pieces B1 and D1) and back side (dark color, pieces A2 and C1).

Beginning at either end, number the pieces in units that connect along the back edge of the ribbon indicated by the dashed lines: A2-A3, B1-B2, C1-C2, etc. The starting piece (A1) can be included in the first unit.

Mark a line down the center of the ribbon—this will help align pieces when pinning and sewing (W).

Add ¼" seam allowance outside the track on both side-s (X's).

Place alignment marks at edges of ribbon where sections overlap (Y's).

At track lines, mark the point where each curve touches the line (Z's).

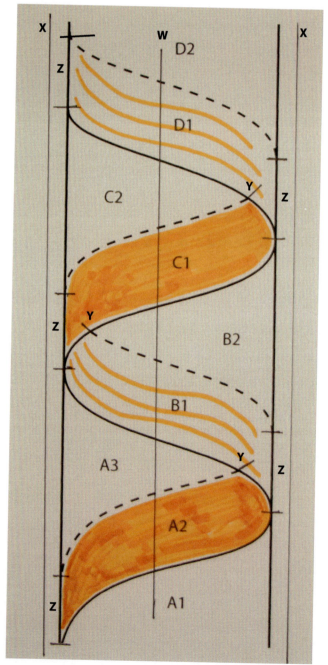

1

2. Cut out the ribbon and background pieces. Place templates face down on the back of the fabric. Place track edges of background pieces on the grain of the fabric. Trace around the templates to mark the seam line. Transfer all alignment marks to the fabric. Cut out, leaving an approximate ¼" seam allowance on all sides.

3. Sew each ribbon piece to its adjacent background piece. (Use the piecing techniques on page 113.)

Continue building these units along the length of the wave.

4. Join the units.

5. Sew the ribbon track into the larger background area.

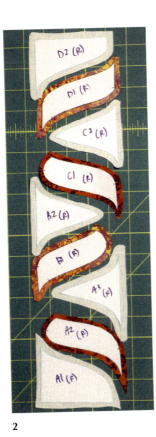

2

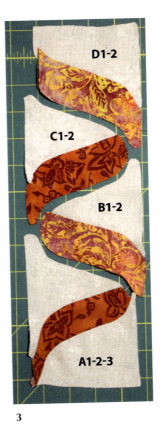

3

4

5

Assembling a Coil

Appliqué or Appliqué-in-a-Track

A coiled ribbon has a back layer and a front layer. Appliqué the back layer first, then the front layer over it.

> This practice template can be found in the online library. See page 3 for address and password.

The photos here show appliqué-in-a-track (AIAT) using raw-edge appliqué (REA) in order to demonstrate the order of adding edge-stitching or trim. The assembly order is the same for raw-edge appliqué (REA) and turned-edge appliqué (TEA), whether or not you are using a track. Raw-edge appliqué can be fused or glued.

1. Mark the template

Color the ribbon to show the back layer (dark color, pieces 1 and 3) and the front layer (light color, pieces 2 and 4).

Number the ribbon pieces in order along the track.

On the ribbon, place alignment marks at edges of ribbon where sections overlap (X's).

AIAT: Add ¼″ seam allowance outside the track on both sides (Y's). Where the ribbon meets the track lines, mark the point where each curve touch the line (Z's).

2. Cut the ribbon and background fabrics. Follow the instructions on page 112 for the appliqué method you are using. Place templates face up on front of fabric.

3. Mark the position of the ribbon pieces on the background fabric with a removable fabric marker.

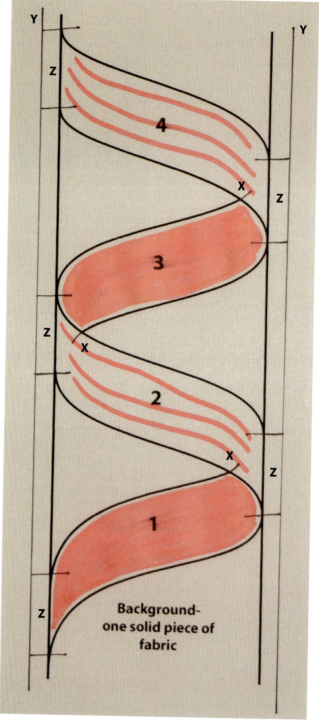

Background— one solid piece of fabric

1

4. Begin with the back layer. Appliqué piece 1.

TEA: Leave unsewn the end that will lie under piece 2 (A).

AIAT: Outer end of ribbon extends to edge of track (B).

4A. REA: Satin stitch or trim along top of piece 1. (If you wish, you can wait and do this as the first part of Step 7.)

5. Appliqué the other back layer pieces (here, piece 3).

TEA: Leave unsewn both ends, because they will lie under top-layer pieces.

6. Appliqué all top-layer pieces (here, pieces 2 and 4).

AIAT: Both raw ends of top layer pieces extend to edge of track.

7. REA: Satin stitch or apply trim along curves that continue from one ribbon segment to the next, and along last ribbon section. Satin-stitching should stay inside the ¼″ seam allowance at the track edges.

8. AIAT: Sew the track into the surrounding area of the quilt.

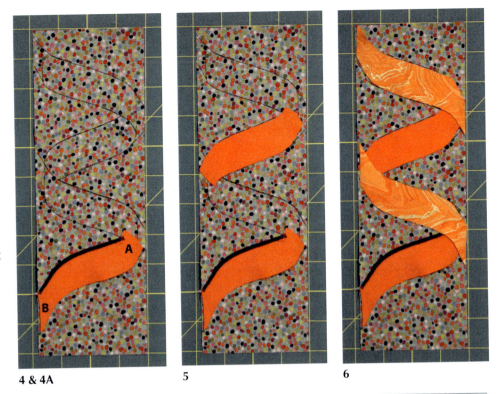

4 & 4A

5

6

7

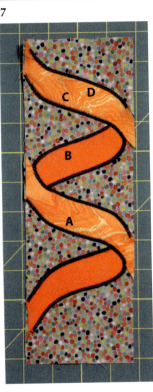

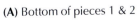

(A) Bottom of pieces 1 & 2
(B) Top of pieces 2 & 3
(C) Bottom of pieces 3 & 4
(D) Top of piece 4

8

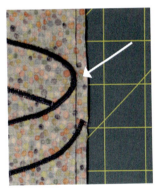

Where satin stitching or trim curves at the side of the track, seam lines should touch but not overlap the stitching.

NOTE: Step 8 can be done before Step 7.

Piecing a Coil

The key to piecing a coil is to think of it in layers. Construct units that set the back layer into the background, then join the units with the top layer ribbon sections.

This practice template can be found in the online library. See page 3 for address and password.

1. Mark the template

Color the ribbon to show the front side (light color, pieces A4 and B4) and back side (dark color, pieces A2 and B2).

Number the pieces in units joining the back layer ribbon sections to their adjacent background pieces (A1-A2-A3, along dashed lines) followed by the next front layer ribbon section (A4, between solid lines). Work along the length of the ribbon continuing in this order.

Mark a line down the center of the ribbon - this will help align pieces when pinning and sewing (W).

On the ribbon, place alignment marks at edges of ribbon where sections overlap (X's).

Add ¼" seam allowance outside the track on both sides (Y's).

Where the ribbon meets the track lines, mark the point where each curve touches the line (Z's).

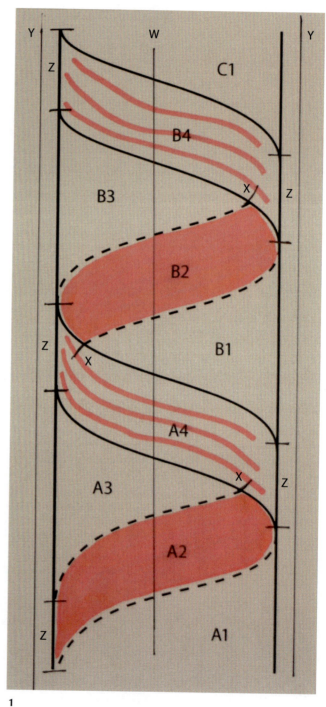

1

2. Cut the ribbon and background pieces. Place templates face down on the back of the fabric. Place track edges of background pieces on the grain of the fabric. Trace around the templates to mark seam lines. Transfer all alignment marks to the fabric. Cut out, leaving an approximate ¼″ seam allowance on all sides.

3. Sew together bottom layer units. (Use the piecing techniques on page 113.)

4. Sew top layer pieces to bottom layer units below them.

5. Join units to complete the coil.

6. Sew the ribbon track into the larger background area

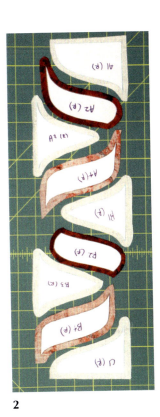

2

3

4

5

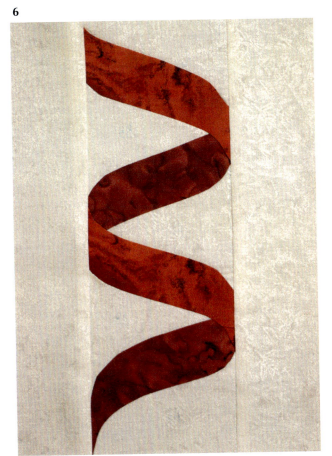

6

Assembling a Double Wave

Appliqué or Appliqué-in-a-Track

Like a single wave, a double wave is constructed in layers. Depending on how you interweave the two ribbons, the order of the layers will vary. Use this example as a guide. Before beginning this, read and understand the instructions for appliquéing a single wave on pages 114-115.

> This practice template can be found in the online library. See page 3 for address and password.

> The photos here show appliqué-in-a-track (AIAT) using raw-edge appliqué (REA) in order to demonstrate the order of adding edge-stitching or trim. The assembly order is the same for raw-edge appliqué (REA) and turned-edge appliqué (TEA), whether or not you are using a track. Raw-edge appliqué can be fused or glued.

1. Mark the template.

Color each ribbon to show its front side (light) and back side (dark).

Number the ribbon pieces in groups that form an X, from the lower layer to the top layer: A1-A2-A3, B1-B2-B3 etc. Depending on how you interwove the two ribbons, some top layer pieces may cross from right to left and some from left to right.

On the ribbon, place alignment marks at edges of ribbon where sections overlap (X's).

AIAT: Add ¼″ seam allowance outside the track on both sides (Y's). Where the ribbon meets the track lines, mark the point where each curve touch the line (Z's).

2. Cut the ribbon and background fabrics. Use the instructions on page 112 for the appliqué method you are using. Place templates face up on front of fabric.

3. Mark the position of the ribbon pieces on the background fabric with a removable fabric marker.

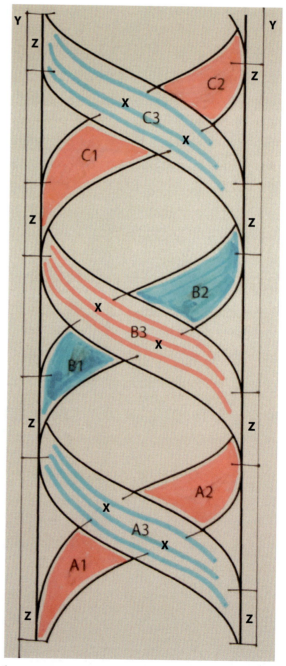

1

4. Begin at whichever end of the wave has the lowest layer. Appliqué bottom layer of the "X".

TEA: Leave unsewn the ends that will lie under top layer sections (A).

AIAT: Outer ends of ribbon sections extend to edge of track (B, C).

5. Appliqué the ribbon piece that forms the top layer of the "X".

AIAT: Both ends of ribbon section extend to edge of track.

6. Repeat steps 4 and 5 to end of ribbon.

7. REA: Satin stitch or trim along all edges that run along only one ribbon section.

8. AIAT: Sew the track into the surrounding background of the quilt.

9. REA: Satin stitch or trim along all remaining ribbon lines. These lines all run along more than one ribbon section. (See Note)

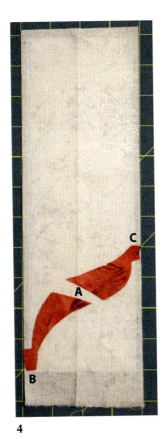

4

5

6

7

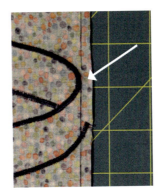

Where satin stitching or trim curves at the side of the track, seam lines should touch but not overlap the stitching.

NOTE: Step 9 can be done before Step 8.

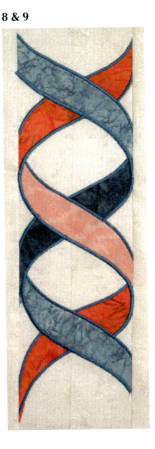

8 & 9

Piecing a Double Wave

When piecing double waves, the back layer must be joined in two units so that one part can go over the front ribbon and the other part can go behind the front ribbon. The order may vary, depending on how you interweave your ribbons. Use this example as a guide.

> This practice template can be found in the online library. See page 3 for address and password.

1. Mark the template

Color each ribbon to show its front side (light) and back side (dark).

Number the pieces in units joining the back layer ribbon sections to their adjacent backgrounds (A1-A2-A3) followed by the next front layer section (A4). Continue up the ribbon numbering in this order (B1-B2-B3-B4-B5 then B6, etc.).

On the ribbon, place alignment marks at edges of ribbon where sections overlap (X's).

Add ¼" seam allowance outside the track on both sides (Y's).

Where the ribbon meets the track lines, mark the point where each curve touches the line (Z's).

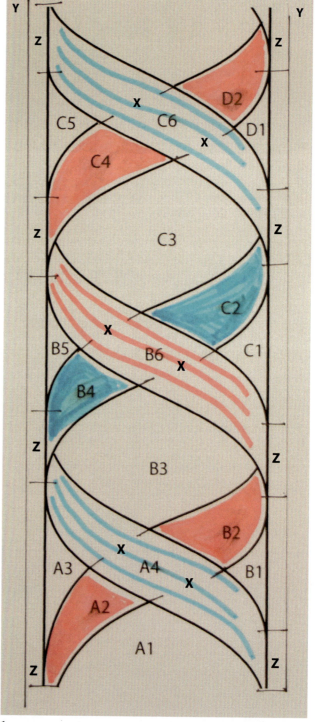

1

2. Cut out the ribbon and background pieces. Place templates face down on the back of the fabric. Place track edges of background pieces on the grain of the fabric. Trace around the templates to mark the seam line. Transfer all alignment marks to the fabric. Cut out, leaving an approximate ¼″ seam allowance on all sides.

3. Sew together bottom layer sections in two units: 1-2-3 and 4-5. (Use piecing techniques on page 111.)

Since A4 is attached completely to unit A1-2-3 it is included in the first unit.

4. Sew bottom layer units 1-2-3 to top layer ribbon sections below. (This is where top layer ribbon crosses over.)

5. Join bottom layer units 4-5 to units 1-2-3. (This is where bottom layer ribbon crosses over top layer ribbon.)

6. Join all units to complete the ribbon.

7. Sew the ribbon track into the larger background area.

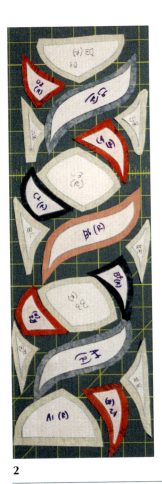

2

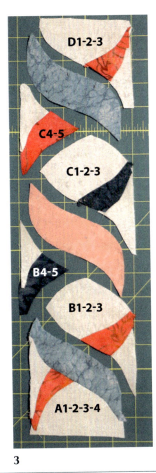

3

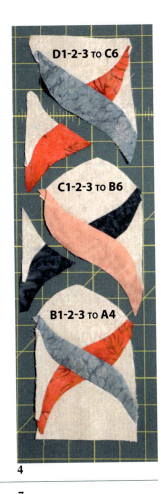

4

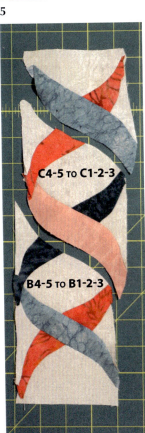

5

6

7

Assembling a Double Coil

Appliqué or Appliqué-in-a-Track

How you interweave and layer a double coil will change the order in which it is assembled. However it might be arranged, start building the coil with the lowest layer and work up to the top layer of the design. Use this example as a guide.

This practice template can be found in the online library. See page 3 for address and password.

The photos here show appliqué-in-a-track (AIAT) using raw-edge appliqué (REA) in order to demonstrate the order of adding edge-stitching or trim. Assembly order is the same for either raw-edge or turned-edge appliqué (TEA), whether or not you are using a track. Raw-edge appliqué can be fused or glued.

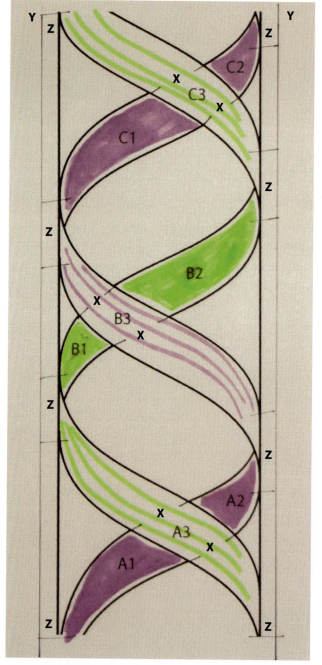

1. Mark the template

Color each ribbon to show the front side (light) and back side (dark).

Number the ribbon pieces in groups that form an X, from the lower layer to the top layer: A1-A2-A3, B1-B2-B3 etc. Depending on how you interwove the two ribbons, some top layer pieces may cross from right to left and some from left to right.

On the ribbon, place alignment marks at edges of ribbon where sections overlap (X's).

AIAT: Add ¼″ seam allowance outside the track on both sides (Y's). Where the ribbon meets the track lines, mark the point where each curve touch the line (Z's).

2. Cut out the ribbon and background fabrics. Follow the instructions on page 112 for the appliqué method you are using. Place templates face up on front of fabric.

3. Mark the position of the ribbon pieces on the background fabric with a removable fabric marker.

4. Appliqué lowest layer pieces.

TEA: Leave unsewn the ends that will lie under upper layers (A).

AIAT: Outer ends of ribbon sections extend to edge of track (B).

5. REA: Satin stitch or trim along edges of ribbon sections that have both ends on the bottom level of the design.

6. Appliqué top layer pieces.

AIAT: Both ends of these pieces extend to edge of track.

7. REA: Satin stitch or trim along edges of pieces on top layer of the design. (See Note) These are all lines that run from one ribbon section to another, except for the outside edges of the end sections, pieces A4 and C6.

8 AIAT: Sew the track into the surrounding background of the quilt.

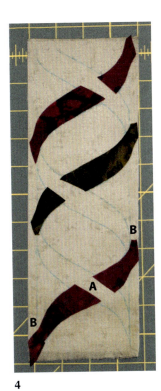

4

5

6

7

8

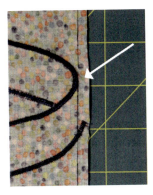

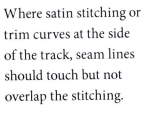

Where satin stitching or trim curves at the side of the track, seam lines should touch but not overlap the stitching.

NOTE: Step 8 can be done before Step 7.

Piecing A Double Coil

Like a single coil, a double coil has layers—there are just more of them. Join the units that set the lower layers into the background, then use the top layer pieces to join the units. How you interweave a double coil will change the order in which it is assembled; use this example as a guide.

This practice template can be found in the online library. See page 3 for address and password.

1. Mark the template

Color each ribbon to show its front side (light) and back side (dark).

Number the pieces in units joining the back layer ribbon sections to their adjacent backgrounds (A1-A2-A3 along dashed lines) followed by the next front layer section (A4 between solid lines). Continue up the ribbon numbering in this order (B1-B2-B3-B4-B5 then B6, etc.).

On the ribbon, place alignment marks at edges of ribbon where sections overlap (X's).

Add ¼" seam allowance outside the track on both sides (Y's).

Where the ribbon meets the track lines, mark the point where each curve touch the line (Z's).

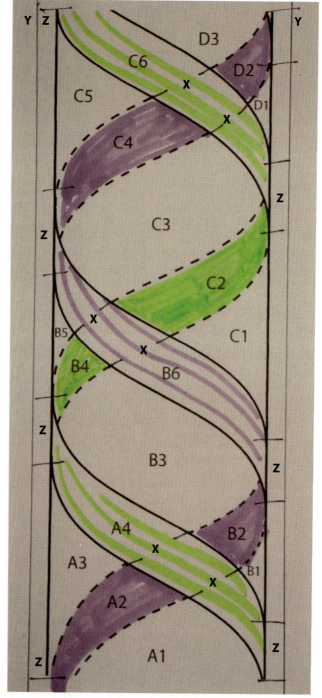

1

2. Cut the ribbon and background pieces. Place templates face down on the back of the fabric. Place track edges of background pieces on the grain of the fabric. Trace around the templates to mark the seam line. Transfer all alignment marks to the fabric. Cut out, leaving an approximate ¼″ seam allowance on all sides.

3. Sew together bottom layer units. (Use the piecing techniques on page 111.)

4. Sew top layer pieces to bottom layer units below them.

5. Join units to complete the coil.

6. Sew the ribbon track into the surrounding background area.

2

3

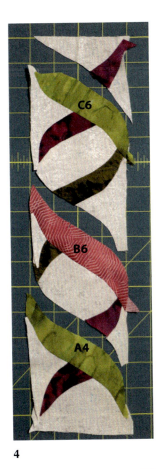

4

5

6

CHAPTER 5

Projects

Here are six simple projects to get you started making sideways spiral quilts. Two are spiral chains, two are ropes and two are ribbons. Each project focuses on a particular aspect of sideways spiral design or construction technique, and each is easily adaptable to different sizes and shapes. Make them as shown, or use them as a starting point for your own creative vision!

Charm Bracelet

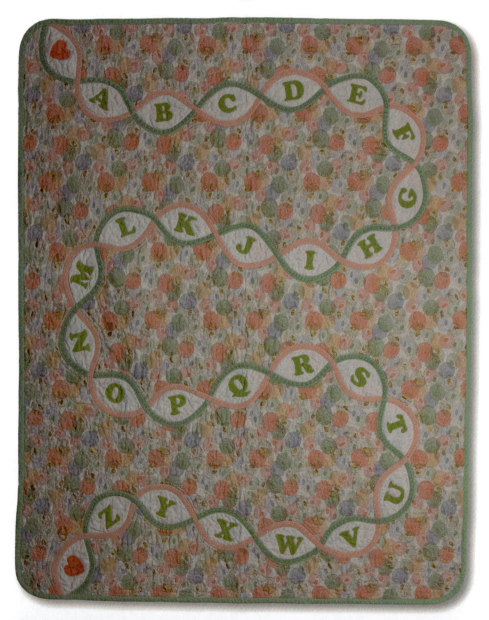

Finished size: 36˝ x 42˝

Create a quilt that sends a message: say "I love you", commemorate a special occasion, honor a special person, remember a vacation, or just express yourself! Charms can be letters or numbers, photos printed on fabric, fussy-cuts from large-scale fabric, found objects or anything else you can imagine and attach to a quilt.

This quilt is quick to make, and easy enough for a child to do with a little help from a friendly adult.

Here's a "don't do what I did" tip: See how the lighter peach bias tape blends into the background? For the chain, be sure to use two fabrics that both stand out from the background so half of the chain doesn't disappear.

MATERIALS & CUTTING LIST

Yardages are based on fabric 42″ wide. All fabrics should be pre-washed and pressed.
See tools lists on pages 93 & 96.

FABRIC	AMOUNT	CUT
Background (Small to medium print)	1⅛ yards	Trim or tear on-grain to 36″ x width of fabric (42″-45″)
Charms (Strong contrast to background)	Enough fabric to cut 28 motifs or 5 sheets printable fabric such as EQ Printables	Iron fusible web to back of this fabric, then use the charm template to cut 28 charms. Alphabet charms can be downloaded from the Sideways Spirals Blog at https://sidewaysspirals.wordpress.com/alphabets-for-charms.
Spiral chain (Solids or tiny monochrome prints in 2 different colors. They should be the same value as each other but should contrast strongly with background so as to be clearly visible over it.)	Fabric 1: ½ yd Fabric 2: ½ yd	From each fabric, cut ¾″ wide bias strips for a total of 180″ of each color. Join strips with diagonal seams to make one continuous strip of each color.
Binding (Can be more of one of the fabrics for the spiral chain, or a different fabric)	½ yard (to allow for bias cut)	Bias strips 2½″ wide for a total of 160″ (Note: Binding must be cut on the bias for round corners. It may be cut on grain if corners of quilt are square.)
Backing	1⅜ yards	No piecing needed. Extra yardage allows for quilting frame.
Batting	1⅛ yards (40″ x 45″)	I like non-flammable batting such as Dream Angel from Quilter's Dream
Fusible web (Light-weight, MUST be paper-backed)	1¼ yards (18″ wide)	
Thread	For sewing background: Match background fabric For making and basting the spiral chain: Water soluble thread, fusible thread or fabric glue (see pages 96-100) For stitching down the spiral chain: Invisible polyester or match bias tape color For decorative stitching over bias tape (optional): Contrasting thread (I like fine polyester or 100-weight silk) For quilting: Coordinate color to background fabric	
⅜″ bias tape maker	If you plan to use fusible web tape get one designed for it (see page 98)	
Optional: Fusible web tape	Use this if you make bias tape with Ironed Method #2 on page 97	
Optional: Fabric glue	Can be used for positioning bias tape (see pages 96-100)	
Removable fabric marker, Optional: Fabric marking pens for coloring letter charms		

INSTRUCTIONS

Make the Charms

1. *If you are cutting charms from fabric:* Copy the charm template onto paper or card stock, then cut out a window. Use this to select and outline your charms with a pencil or pen.

If you are using the printed alphabet charms: Select the letters/numbers/symbols you need. Copy them onto the fabric sheets using the photocopy setting on your printer. Color with fabric markers if desired.

2. Iron fusible web to the back of the charms.

3. Cut out the charms. Do not remove the paper.

Make the Bias Tape

Make ⅜″ bias tape using one of the methods on pages 96-100.

> For the chain outline, instead of using bias tape, you might use decorative trim such as rickrack or gold braid. If you use a bulky trim, you may need a sewing machine foot with a raised groove on the bottom (such as a cording foot) to fit over the trim.

Assemble the Spiral Chain

1. Follow the instructions for assembling a Spiral Chain on pages 101-103.

2. If your sewing machine has an alphabet decorative stitch, stitch the letter of each charm on its surrounding bias tape. (See detail photo - I did letters on the green bias tape and hearts on the pink.) Follow the stitching order for chains shown on page 105.

Quilt and Bind

1. Follow the instructions for quilting a Spiral Chain on pages 106-107.

2. Use a bowl to mark the curved corners. Stitch along the marked line, then trim just outside it.

3. Bind the edges.*

4. Add a hanging sleeve and label if you wish.

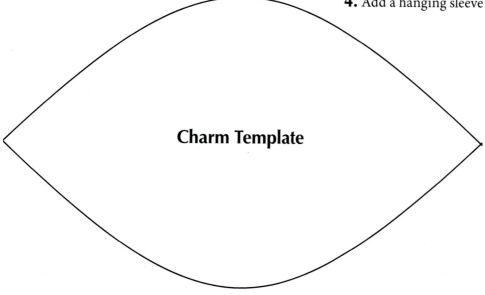

Charm Template

ALTERNATE DESIGN

Here's another version of Charm Bracelet, with pieced charms that look like DNA. The charms could have been foundation pieced, but I took an easier route: I pieced several strip-sets, then cut out the charms. I even pieced together the leftovers to make some of the charms for more variety.

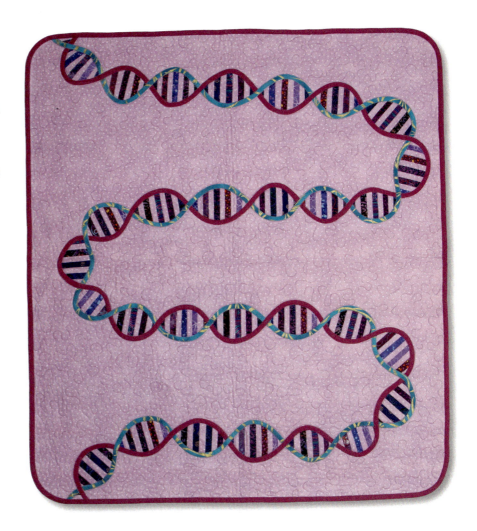

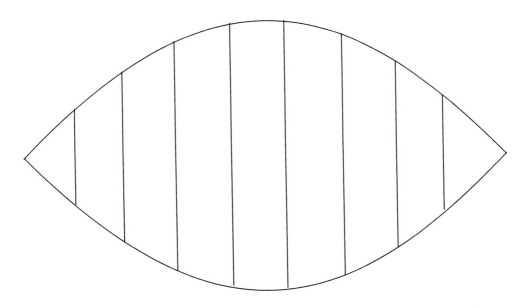

* If you're not familiar with traditional binding technique, see instructions on the Spiromaniacs blog at http://spiromaniacs.files.wordpress.com/2008/09/binding-a-quilt.pdf.

Flying Free

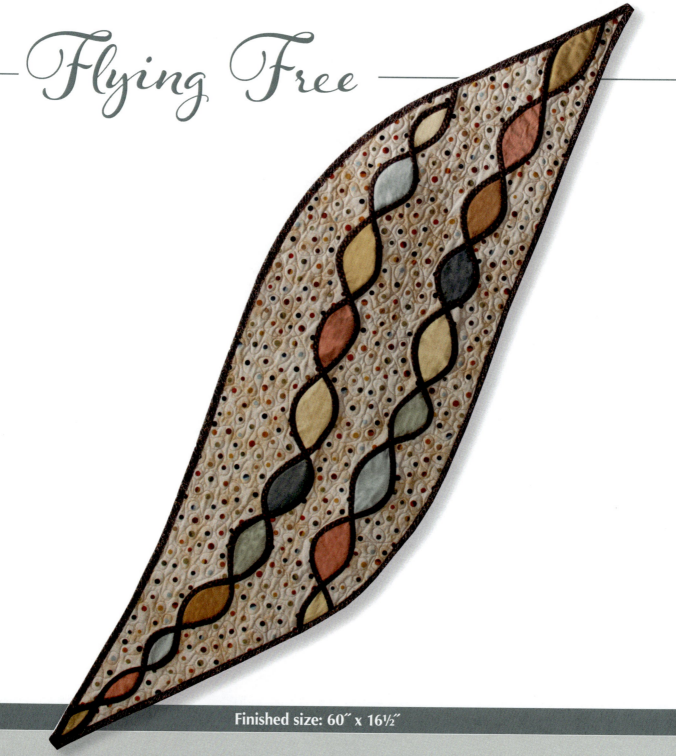

Finished size: 60″ x 16½″

This table runner was one of the very first spiral chain quilts I made when I was just figuring out the process. It hung on my design wall for a couple of years until I decided that yes, it should go in the book. It was made with the freeform charm technique on page 18.

Use the template on page 138 to make this any size you wish. You can use that template to create the freeform charms, or draw your own.

MATERIALS & CUTTING LIST

Yardages are based on fabric 42″ wide. All fabrics should be pre-washed and pressed.
See tools lists on pages 93 & 96.

FABRIC	AMOUNT	CUT
Background (Small to medium-sized print)	1 yard	Cut in half (in either direction) and join pieces end-to-end.
Charms (A variety of solid colors)	Enough to cut 20 charms approx. 3″ x 5″ each	Iron fusible web to back of these fabrics, then use charm templates to cut 20 charms.
Bias tape (Solid or tiny monochrome print in 1 or 2 colors. Should contrast strongly with background so as to be clearly visible over it. If using two fabrics, they should be the same value as each other.)	½ yard*	Cut ¾″ wide bias strips for a total of 240″ or 120″ of each of 2 colors.
Binding (Can be the same fabric as the spiral chain, or a different fabric)	½ yard*	Cut bias strips 2½″ wide for a total of 160″. Join strips with diagonal seams to make one continuous strip.
Backing	1 yard	Cut in half (in either direction) and join pieces end-to-end, same as Background fabric.
Batting	18″ x 64″ piece	
Fusible web (Light-weight, MUST be paper-backed)	½ yard (18″ wide)	
Thread		For sewing background: Match background fabric For making and basting the spiral chain: Water soluble thread, fusible thread or fabric glue (see pages 96-100) For stitching down the spiral chain: Invisible polyester or match bias tape color For decorative stitching over bias tape (optional): Contrasting thread (I like fine polyester or 100-weight silk) For quilting: Coordinate color to background fabric
⅜″ bias tape maker		If you plan to use fusible web tape get one designed for it (see page 98)
Optional: Fusible web tape		Use this if you make bias tape with Ironed Method #2 on page 97
Optional: Fabric glue		Can be used for positioning bias tape (see pages 96-100)
Removable fabric marker		
If you manually enlarge the template on page 139: Freezer paper, newsprint or art paper 30″ x 62″		

* ½ yard will leave you with extra fabric, but it gives you long enough pieces to avoid having too many seams.

If bias tape and binding fabrics are the same ½ yard is enough for all.

INSTRUCTIONS

Download and assemble full-size templates from the online library (see page 3) or enlarge the grid at right to create a full-size template. (Draw the grid with squares of your desired size on freezer paper or large sheets of art paper. For the sample shown on page 136 the squares should be 3″. Copy the contents of each square of the diagram into the corresponding square on your paper.) Once you have a full-size template, make a second copy, then take a picture or make another copy of any size for reference.

Prepare the background

1. Assemble the background fabric (see cutting list).

2. Lay a full-size template over the fabric and pin around the edges (or iron, if you're using freezer paper). Cut the background fabric around the outside edge of the template.

3. Re-pin the template to the background fabric *between* the chains at the X's. Remove the pins around the outside edge.

4. Cut away the template along the center lines of the chains. Do not cut the fabric underneath.

5. With the removable marker, draw a line on the background fabric along each cut edge to mark the center lines of the two chains. Remove the template from the background fabric.

6. Mark the Right and Left ends of the background.

Prepare the charms

1. Cut out the charm templates from the second copy of the template.

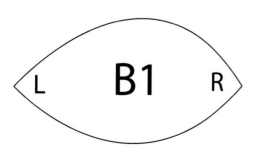

2. Trace each charm onto the FRONT of its corresponding fabric.

3. Iron fusible web to the back of the charms.

4. After fusing, mark each charm with its number and its left and right points (see example below). (Don't do this before fusing, as sometimes heat will permanently set or erase removable marker ink.)

Prepare the bias tape

Cut ¾″ wide bias strips for the chains. Join them end-to-end with diagonal seams to make four strips 60" long. Use one of the methods on pages 96-100 to make bias tape.

Assemble the chains

1. Arrange the charms on the background along their respective center lines. Keep them in numerical order. Keep the Left points to the left and Right points to the right.

2. Remove the paper backing and fuse the charms into place. (Cover them with scratch paper or a pressing sheet to protect your iron.)

3. Outline the charms with the bias tape, following the instructions on pages 102-103. Temporarily anchor the bias tape to the background according to whichever method you used for making bias tape.

4. Optional: Add decorative stitching over the bias tape (page 107). You may have already done this when you made the bias tape if you used Sewing Machine Method #3 on page 100.

Quilt and bind

1. Layer the top, batting and back. Quilt, using one of the methods on pages 106-107.

2. Trim away excess batting and backing, then bind edges to finish. (Binding instructions can be found on the Spiromaniacs Blog at http://spiromaniacs.files.wordpress.com/2008/09/binding-a-quilt.pdf.)

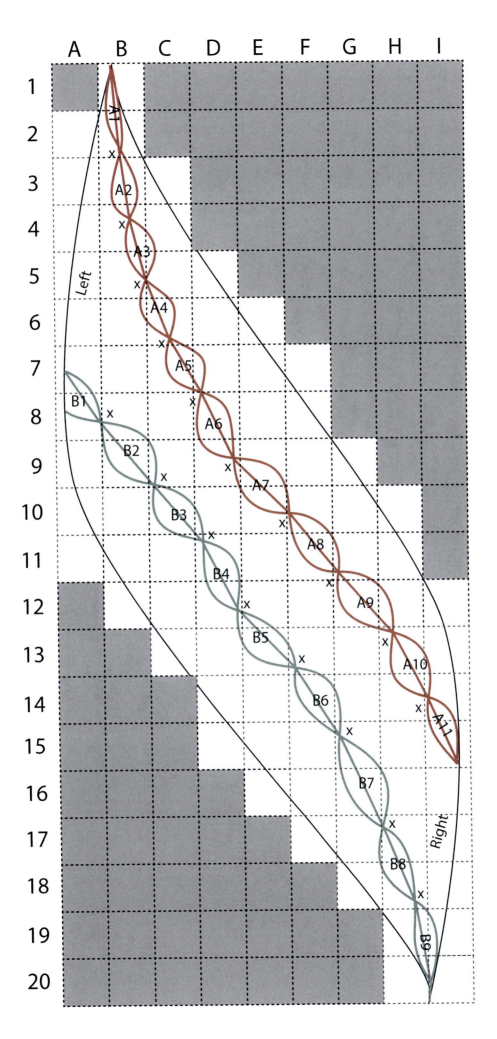

Rope Runner

Finished size:

Bed runner: 18˝ x 84˝

Table runner: 18˝ x 58˝ with two place mats 18˝ x 13˝

This runner can be used on the foot of a bed or on a table. To make placemats, cut off pieces after quilting and bind them individually.

MATERIALS & CUTTING LIST

Yardages are based on fabric 42″ wide. All fabrics should be pre-washed and pressed.
See tools lists on pages 93 & 96.

FABRIC	AMOUNT	CUT
Background (Small to medium size print, or solid)	1⅛ yards	Cut or tear on-grain across width of fabric for 2 pieces 18″ x WOF, then sew selvage edges together to make one piece 18″ wide by 84″ long. (Extra yardage allows for straightening)
Rope Colors 1 & 2, Side Twists (Two different colors similar in value. Monochrome textures or small dense prints that pick up colors in background fabric. They need to contrast enough with the background to be clearly visible over it.)	⅜ yd each of two fabrics	Cut first: From each fabric, cut bias strips ¾″ wide for a total of 90″. Using diagonal seams, sew the strips together to make 1 strip 90″ long of each fabric. Or, if you wish, you can make 2 strips of alternating colors. From each fabric cut 13 Rope Sections after fusing.
Rope Outline, Side Twists (Solid or tiny tone-on-tone print or texture)	½ yard	Cut bias strips ¾″ wide for a total of 500″. Using diagonal seams, sew the strips together to make 2 strips 90″ long. Sew together the rest of the strips into one long strip.
Binding (Can be more of one of the rope section or side twist fabrics, or a different fabric)	½ yard	Cut strips 2½″ wide for a total of 310″. May be cut bias or on-grain. Join strips with bias seams to make one strip 170″ long (for table runner) and two strips 70″ long (for placemats). For a bed runner, make one strip 220″ long.
Backing	1¼ yards	Cut or tear on-grain across width of fabric for 2 pieces 22″ x WOF, then sew selvage edges together to make one piece 22″ wide by 84″ long. (Extra yardage allow for quilting frame.)
Batting	20″ x 84″	I like non-flammable batting such as Dream Angel from Quilter's Dream
Fusible web (Light-weight, MUST be paperbacked)	1 yard (18″ wide)	
Thread		For sewing background: Match background fabric For making and basting the spiral chain: Water soluble thread, fusible thread or fabric glue (see pages 96-100) For stitching down the spiral chain: Invisible polyester or match bias tape color For decorative stitching over bias tape (optional): Contrasting thread (I like fine polyester or 100-weight silk) For quilting: Coordinate color to background fabric
⅜″ bias tape maker		If you plan to use fusible web tape get one designed for it (see page 98)
Optional: Fusible web tape		Use this if you make bias tape with Ironed Method #2 on page 97
Optional: Fabric glue		Can be used for positioning bias tape (see pages 96-100)
Removable fabric marker		

INSTRUCTIONS

Prepare the Rope Sections

1. Trace the Rope Section template onto the paper of the fusible web. Make 13 rope sections from each color—26 sections total. (Note: The template here is in reverse so that the rope will twist as shown in the photograph when it is assembled.)

2. Iron the fusible web with traced rope sections to the back of the two rope fabrics—13 on each color.

3. Cut out the rope sections but do not remove the paper yet.

Prepare the Background

1. Cut or tear background fabric across width of fabric for 2 pieces 18″ x WOF, then sew selvage edges together to make one piece 18″ wide by 84″ long.

2. Mark or press a line lengthwise down the center. You can use any type of pen or pencil, as this line, and the ones in Step 3, will be completely covered.

3. Mark two more lines 3¼″ from each lengthwise edge.

Make the Bias Tape

Using the Rope Outline fabric and the Side Twist fabrics, make ⅜″ bias tape using one of the methods on pages 96-100. Refer to the cutting list for lengths.

Assemble the Rope

Arrange the rope sections along the center line of the background. Follow the instructions on page 104 to fuse them into place and outline them with the bias tape.

Add the Side Twists

1. To mark the placement of the side twists, use a straightedge and the removable marker. Place the straight edge across each narrow point of the rope, extending across and perpendicular to the lines that you marked 3¼″ from the long edges of the runner. Mark a 1″ line across the side line where the straight edge and the side line cross. (See diagram on facing page)

2. Use one 90″ strip of rope outline bias tape and one 90″ strip of rope section bias tape. Beginning at the end of the table runner, lay the two bias tapes side-by-side at the first crossing line. (A in diagram at right.) Pin across the bias tapes at the line.

3. Cross the left bias tape over the right bias tape and lay them side-by-side in the new order at the next line crossing (B). Pin into place at the line. (If you are using fabric glue, glue them into place; if you are stitching with water soluble thread or fusible thread, pin now then go back and stitch down later.)

4. Again cross the left bias tape over the right bias tape and lay them side-by-side in the new order at the next line crossing (C). Pin or glue into place.

5. Continue crossing and pinning bias tape strips to the end of the runner.

6. Repeat for the other side of the runner.

7. If you are using water-soluble thread, zigzag down each bias strip to hold it securely in place. If you are using fusible tape or fusible thread, iron the bias tape into place now.

8. Optional: Add decorative stitching over the center of the bias tape (see page 105). (You may have already done this when you made the bias tape, if you used Sewing Machine Method #3 on page 100).

Quilt, Cut Placemats and Bind

1. Layer the top, batting and back. Quilt, using one of the methods on pages 106-107.

2. For placemats, cut off two or more sections 13″ long.

3. Bind edges to finish. (Binding instructions can be found on the Spiromaniacs Blog at http://spiromaniacs.files.wordpress.com/2008/09/binding-a-quilt.pdf.)

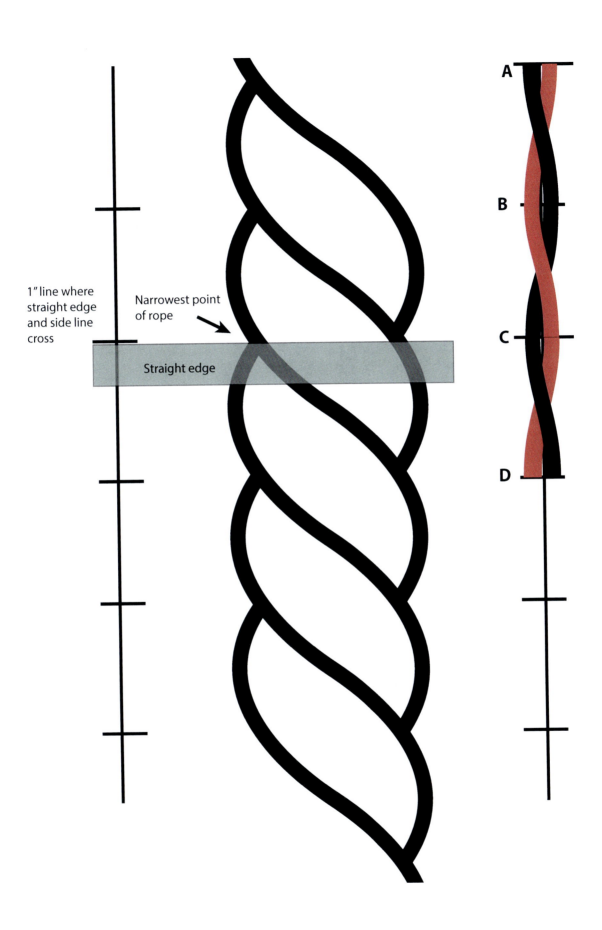

1" line where straight edge and side line cross

Narrowest point of rope

Straight edge

A

B

C

D

Rope Section Templates

Templates shown here are 90% of full size (in order to fit them on the page). Here are three options for making them full size:

1. Download full-size templates at: https://sidewaysspirals.wordpress.com/project-templates.

2. Copy and enlarge 111%.

3. Use them at this size. They will make a slightly smaller rope and you will need a few more rope sections than the 26 in the instructions.

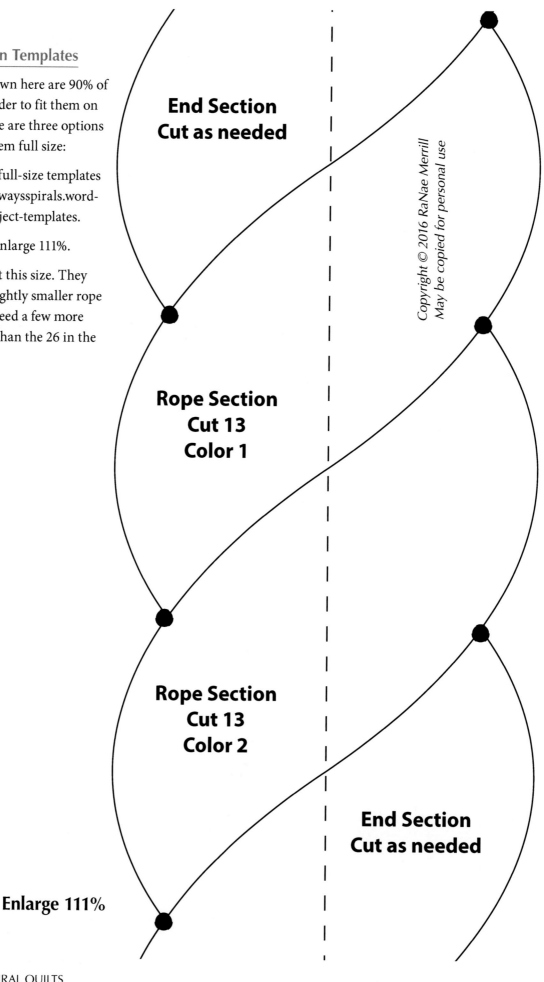

**End Section
Cut as needed**

**Rope Section
Cut 13
Color 1**

**Rope Section
Cut 13
Color 2**

**End Section
Cut as needed**

Enlarge 111%

Optional template

If you would like to adjust this design to make the rope run in two directions, use this template to change direction. Enlarge per instructions on page 144. Refer to the drawing exercises on pages 40-41 for more information.

Enlarge 111%

Rope & Compass

Finished size: 42″ x 42″

A mariner's compass and a rope ring combine to create this quilt with a nautical feel. Fusing makes the assembly easy. In order to manage the bulk of the bias tape at its points, the compass is built on a separate piece of background fabric, then set into a circle in the main background, so choose a background fabric with an unstructured design than can hide the seam.

MATERIALS & CUTTING LIST

Yardages are based on fabric 42″ wide. All fabrics should be pre-washed and pressed.
See tools lists on pages 93 & 96.

FABRIC	AMOUNT	CUT
Rope Color 1 (Dark rope sections, B points of Compass)	½ yard	16 Rope Section Reverse Template 8 Compass Piece B
Rope Color 2 (Light rope sections, A points and Center of Compass)	½ yard	16 Rope Section Reverse Template 8 Compass Piece A 1 Compass Center
Background (This should be a non-directional small- to medium-sized print that will not show an obvious break in the pattern when cut)	2 yards	Main Background: 1 square using WOF as dimension (ex: 42″ WOF = 42″ x 42″ square) Compass Background: 22″ x 22″ square
Bias Tape & Binding	1 yard (allows for cutting bias)	Bias tape: 600″ of ½″ wide bias strips Binding: 190″ of strips 2½″ wide. If you plan to finish the table topper as a square they can be cut on grain; if round, they must be cut on the bias.
Backing	1¼ yds	Extra yardage allows for quilting frame
Batting	42″ square	I like non-flammable batting such as Dream Angel from Quilter's Dream
Fusible web (Wonder Under or similar, lightweight, MUST be paper-backed)	1 yard (18″ wide)	
Thread		For sewing background: Match background fabric For making and basting the spiral chain: Water soluble thread, fusible thread or fabric glue (see pages 96-100) For stitching down the spiral chain: Invisible polyester or match bias tape color For quilting: Coordinate color to background fabric
¼″ bias tape maker		If you plan to use fusible web tape get one designed for it (see page 98)
Optional: Fusible web tape		Use this if you make bias tape with Ironed Method #2 on page 97
Optional: Fabric glue		Can be used for positioning bias tape (see pages 96-100)
Fabric marker removable with heat, suc as Bohin pencil or Frixion pen		

INSTRUCTIONS

Prepare Rope Sections

1. Trace 32 copies of the Reverse Rope Section Template (page 152) onto the paper side of fusible web. Include the lines; mark the dashed line as a dashed line to identify the outside edge of the rope circle.

2. Iron marked fusible web to the back of Rope Color 1 and Rope Color 2 fabrics: 16 Rope Sections on each fabric. Fuse according to manufacturer's instructions. Cut out rope sections. Do not remove paper.

3. Print a copy of the Rope Sections Face-up Template. Lay each cut-out rope section on the front of the rope section and mark the dots on the edges of the fabric with a removable fabric marker.

Prepare Bias Tape

Using one of the methods on pages 96-100, make 600″ of ¼″ bias tape.

Prepare the Main Background

1. Measure the width of the Background fabric from selvage to selvage (it will be between 40″ and 44″). Square up one end, then cut the length of the fabric same as the width to make a square.

2. Press the background square vertically, horizontally and diagonally in both directions. Make sure these lines all pass through the same center point.

3. Measure and mark 18″ from the center point along each pressed line with a removable marker.

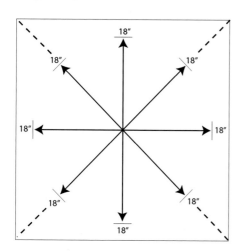

Make the Compass

1. Trace 8 copies of Compass Piece A onto the paper side of fusible web. Fuse to back of Rope 2 fabric.

2. Trace 8 copies of Compass Piece B onto paper side of fusible web. Fuse to back of Rope 1 fabric.

3. Trace 1 Compass Center onto paper side of fusible web. Fuse to back of Rope 2 fabric.

4. Cut out compass pieces and center.

5. Cut a 22″ square of Background fabric. Press it in half vertically, horizontally and diagonally in both directions (as you did with the Main Background) to mark placement lines.

6. Remove paper from Center circle. Fold vertically and horizontally to find the center point. Place it on the background, aligning it with pressed lines. Do not iron yet.

7. Remove paper from Compass Piece A's. Position around Center, aligning points with pressed lines on background. Bottom edge of pieces should lie against Center but not overlap.

8. Remove paper from Compass Piece B's. Position between Compass Piece A's. Bottom edge of pieces should lie against Compass Piece A's but not overlap.

9. Fuse all pieces into place according to manufacturer's directions.

10. Temporarily position bias tape over edges of Compass sections using the method you chose on pages 96-100. Work in this order:

   1. Piece B's: Cover long edges. Trim inside ends of bias tape even with edge of Piece A's. Bias tape will overlap at outside tips.

   2. Piece A's. Cover long edges. Trim inside ends of bias tape even with edge of Center Circle. Be sure to cover ends of Piece B strips. Bias tape will overlap at outside tips.

   3. Center Circle: Cover edge. Be sure to cover ends of Piece A strips.

Templates for this project can also be downloaded at
https://sidewaysspirals.wordpress.com/project-templates

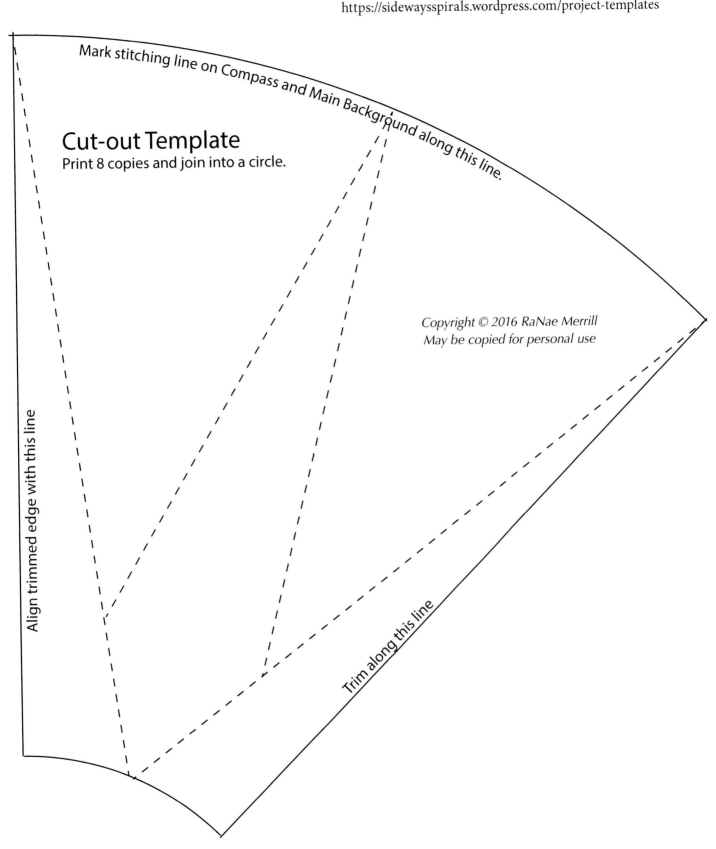

Mark stitching line on Compass and Main Background along this line.

Cut-out Template
Print 8 copies and join into a circle.

Copyright © 2016 RaNae Merrill
May be copied for personal use

Align trimmed edge with this line

Trim along this line

Assemble Compass and Background

1. Print 8 copies of the Cut-out Template (page 149), cut them out and join them into a circle.

2. *Mark the seam line on the Compass:* Lay the Cut-out Template over the Compass, aligning it with the points and with the edge of the center circle (A). Using the removable fabric marker, trace the outside edge of the circle to mark the stitching line.

3. Trim the Compass ¼″ OUTSIDE the marked stitching line (B).

4. *Mark the seam line on the Main Background:* Pin the Cut-out Template circle over the Main Background, aligning the pressed lines with the template (C). Pin securely. Using the removable fabric marker, trace the outside edge to mark the stitching line. Remove template.

5. Sew a line of basting stitches along the marked line on the Main Background, using thread that matches the fabric (D).

6. Cut out the center of the Main Background ¼″ INSIDE the basted stitching line (D).

7. Clip the seam allowance every 1″ between the cut edge and the basting line; do not clip stitches.

8. Turn under the seam allowance of the Main Background with the stitching just hidden under the edge of the fold. Pin or baste ⅛″ from fold.

9. *Insert the Compass into the Main Background:* Lay the Compass face up. Lay the Main Background face up over it, aligning the points of the Compass with pressed lines on the Main Background. Align the marked seam line on the Compass with the folded edge of the Main Background. Pin or baste securely.

10. Using matching or invisible thread, blindstitch along the folded edge of the Main Background by hand or with a narrow machine zigzag. Remove basting if necessary.

Build the Rope

1. Remove the paper backing from a Rope section and lay it on the Background with its outside edge touching any 18″ mark (E). (The dashed line on the paper backing indicates the outside edge.)

2. Add the next Rope Section in the other color using the marked dots to align the sections.

3. Position Rope Sections around the circle, alternating colors. Each time you reach an 18″ mark, align the Rope Sections to the mark. Adjust the Rope Sections between marks if necessary to make an even circle, but do not leave space between the sections.

4. Once you are happy with the placement of the Rope Sections, fuse them into place.

5. Outline the rope with bias tape (see page 104). Anchor it temporarily using the same method that you used on the compass.

Quilt and Bind

1. Layer the top, batting and back. Quilt, using one of the methods on pages 106-107.

2. If you wish, trim the outside edge of the quilt to make a circle. (If you do, binding must be cut on the bias.)

3. Bind edges to finish. (Binding instructions can be found on the Spiromaniacs Blog at http://spiromaniacs.files.wordpress.com/2008/09/binding-a-quilt.pdf.)

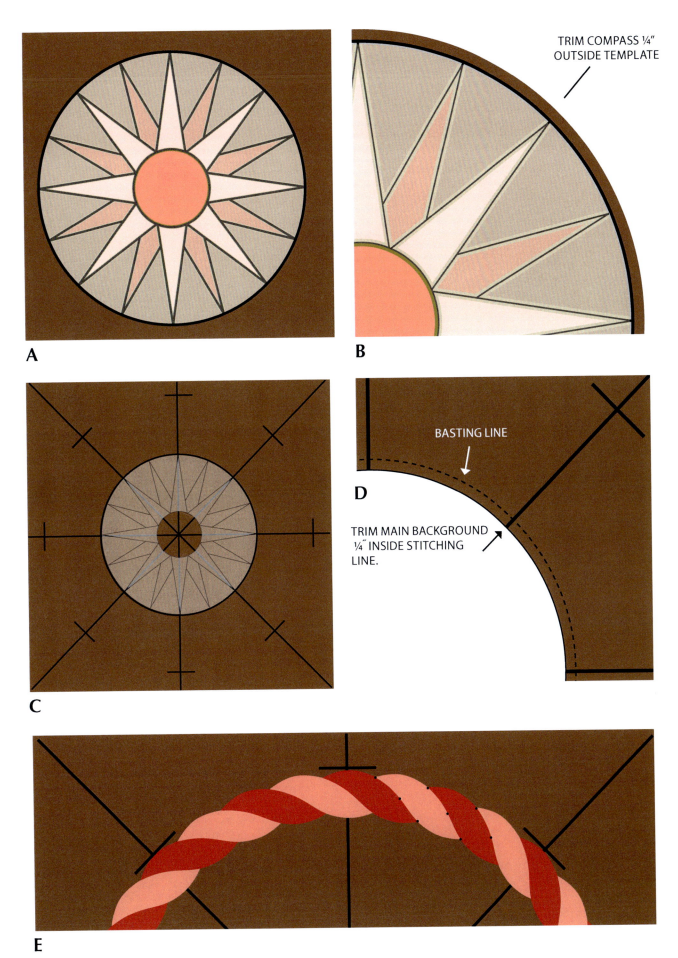

A

B

TRIM COMPASS ¼″
OUTSIDE TEMPLATE

C

D

BASTING LINE

TRIM MAIN BACKGROUND
¼″ INSIDE STITCHING
LINE.

E

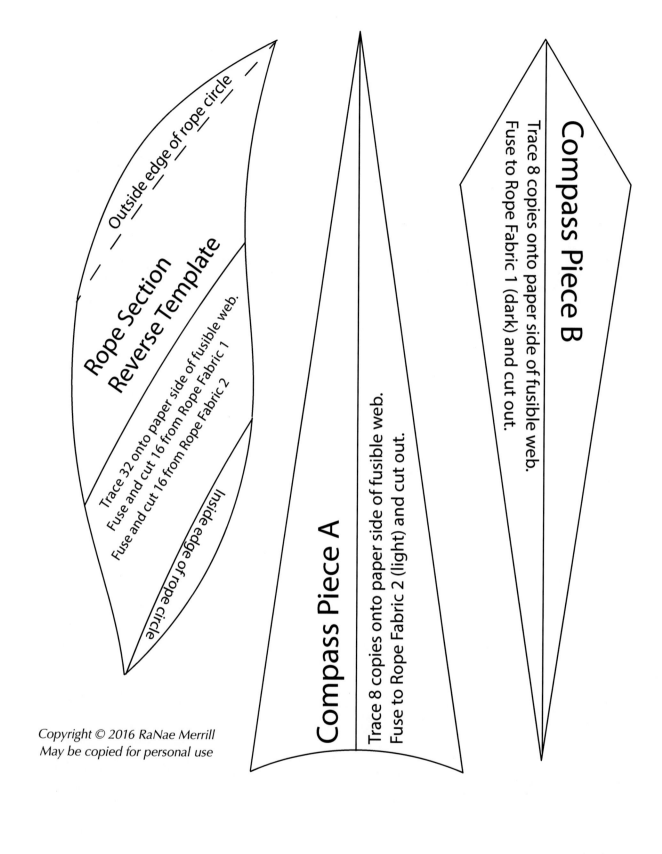

Outside edge of rope circle

Rope Section Reverse Template

Trace 32 onto paper side of fusible web.
Fuse and cut 16 from Rope Fabric 1
Fuse and cut 16 from Rope Fabric 2

Inside edge of rope circle

Compass Piece A

Trace 8 copies onto paper side of fusible web.
Fuse to Rope Fabric 2 (light) and cut out.

Compass Piece B

Trace 8 copies onto paper side of fusible web.
Fuse to Rope Fabric 1 (dark) and cut out.

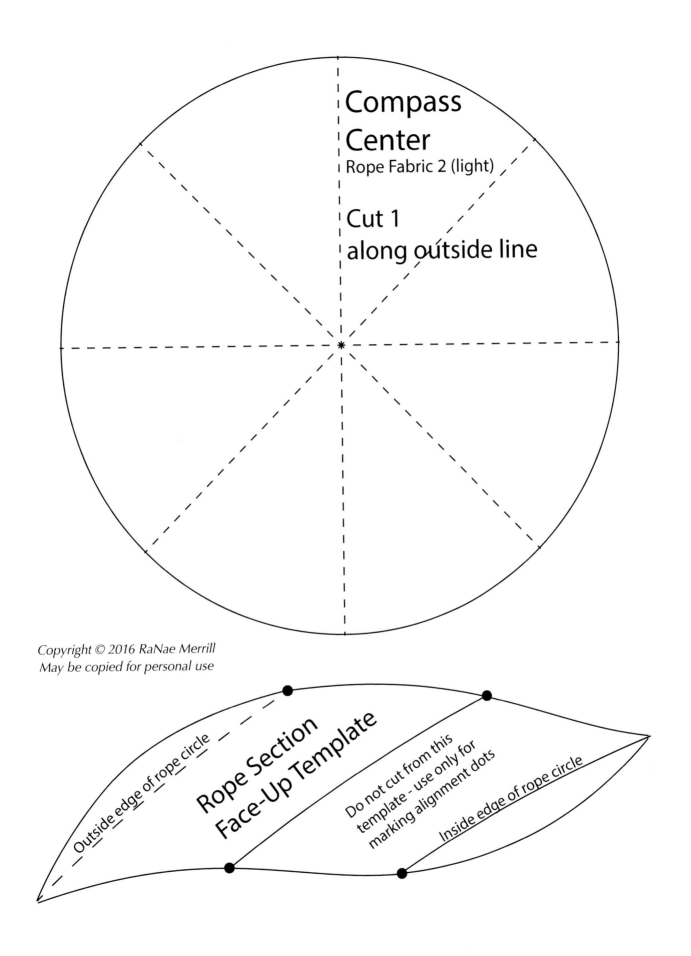

Compass Center
Rope Fabric 2 (light)

Cut 1
along outside line

Outside edge of rope circle

Rope Section
Face-Up Template

Do not cut from this
template - use only for
marking alignment dots

Inside edge of rope circle

Built-in Bookmark
BOOK COVER

Finished size: This pattern is written for an 8¼″ x 10¾″ magazine (like American Quilter), but see instructions for measuring to fit any book.

This book cover has a faux ribbon bookmark on the cover, but still has a real one inside. The quilting makes it appear embossed like a luxurious leather-bound book.

MATERIALS & CUTTING LIST

Yardages are based on fabric 42″ wide. All fabrics should be pre-washed and pressed.
See tools list on page 109.

FABRIC	AMOUNT	CUT
Outside Cover (Solid)	½ yard	1 piece 6¼″ x 12″ (front outside cover) 1 piece 11″ x 12″ (back and spine outside cover) 1 piece 1¾″ x 12″ (background of ribbon) 2 pieces 6½″ x 12″ (inside pockets for book cover) 2 pieces 7″ x 1½″ (top/bottom facings)
Ribbon (A light and a dark value of the same color. Monochrome textures or small dense prints. If one is a print, the other should be solid. They need to contrast enough with the background to be clearly visible over it.)	5″ square of two fabrics	From dark fabric cut Ribbon Sections 1, 3, 5 (Template pg. 157) From light fabric cut Ribbon Sections 2 & 4. Use cutting instructions for Appliqué-in-a-Track on page 112. Adhere templates face up on front of fabric using double-sided tape. Cut after fusing, if you use fusible web.
Interior Lining (Any color or pattern)	¼ yard (must be a Fat Qtr)	1 piece 18″ x 12″
Ribbon (1″ wide, any color)	12″	
Batting	18″ x 12″	Choose a flat, dense batting such as Hobbs 80/20, not a puffy polyester or wool
Fusible web (optional) (Light-weight, MUST be paperbacked)	Two 5″ squares	
Thread		For assembly: Match background fabric For satin stitch on edges of ribbon: Coordinating color silk or shiny polyester For quilting: Match background fabric
Optional: Fabric glue		Can be used for positioning ribbon sections instead of fusible web
Removable fabric marker, permanent double-sided tape		

To adjust size for any book:

Measure the height of the book and add 1¼″.

Measure around the book from the edge of the front cover to the edge of the back cover and add 1¼″.

These measurements allow for a ¼″ seam around the outside edge, plus some shrinkage when quilting, plus the thickness of a hard-bound book cover.

Position the ribbon track ½″ to 1″ from the left side of the front cover. Remember to account for the thickness of the spine when figuring the position of the ribbon.

INSTRUCTIONS

1. Assemble the ribbon using the instructions on pages 118-119 for assembling a coil with raw edge appliqué-in-a-track.

2. Sew the Front Outside Cover to the right side of the ribbon track. Sew the Back Outside Cover to the left side of the ribbon track (A).

3. Draw a border line 1½″ from the edge all the way around the book cover. Draw a second border line 1/4″ inside this one (B1 & 2).

4. Trace the quilting designs onto the front cover of the book (B3 & 4).

5. Layer the inside lining, batting and book cover. Quilt the center medallion and corner ornaments, then the border lines. Fill in the rest of the front and back cover with parallel lines ¼″ apart (B).

6. Diagonally clip the batting only (not the fabric) at each corner just inside the crossed seam lines (C). (This reduces bulk when the corner is turned right side out.)

7. Hem one long edge of both Inside Pocket pieces. Pin them face down on front of book cover with raw edge along ends of book cover (D7).

8. Position ribbon at top edge of book cover where the ribbon on the front meets the top edge (D8).

9. Hem one long edge of Top/Bottom Facing pieces.

10. Position the Top/Bottom facings face down on front of book cover between inside pocket pieces. Ends of facings overlap the inside pocket piece (D10).

11. Stitch all the way around the book cover with a ¼″ seam (D11). Do not clip corners. Test fit. If necessary re-stitch the outside seam for better fit.

12. Turn book cover right side out. At corners, fold fabric and use the bulk of the folded fabric to push the point out, stabilizing the corner.

13. Press well and insert your book.

Happy reading!

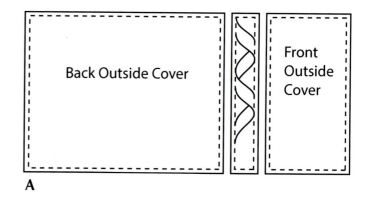

A

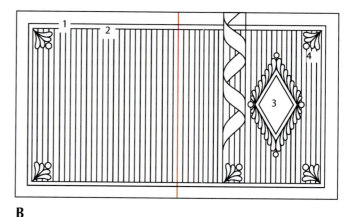

B

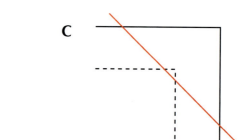

C

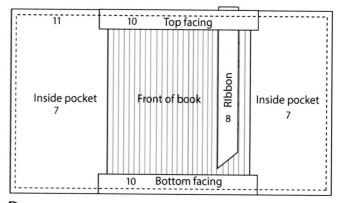

D

Ribbon Template

Cut fabric for ribbon and background according to instructions on page 110 for appliqué-in-a-track

Quilting Templates

Trace onto book cover with a removable fabric marker.
Use a light box or tape the paper and the fabric on a window.

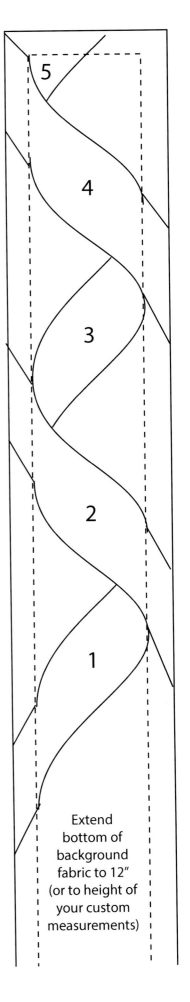

5

4

3

2

1

Extend bottom of background fabric to 12" (or to height of your custom measurements)

I Love You to Infinity

Finished sizes:
Bed runner: 19" x 82"
Pillow sham: 27" x 18" (standard pillow)

Although this bed runner looks and is constructed like a double coil, because the ends loop around it is actually a single ribbon loop. This is why there are only two colors—one for the front of the ribbon, one for the back. Notice that the loop on the end of this runner is different from the corner ribbons on page 78. Those have two turns of the ribbon, this has just one and so it changes which side of the ribbon appears. To make this type of ribbon, draw two loops side-by-side.

BONUS PATTERN:
INFINITY PILLOW
Go to the Sideways Spirals *Blog for download—*
see page 3 for address.
Duvet cover pattern also available in my online store
(see Resources, page 162).

MATERIALS & CUTTING LIST

Yardages are based on fabric 42″ wide. All fabrics should be pre-washed and pressed.

See tools list on page 109.

FABRIC	AMOUNT	CUT
Background (Solid white)	1¼ yds	All background templates For piecing: All background templates. Place template face down on back of fabric, trace around it, copy alignment marks in seam allowance, cut ¼″ outside of traced line. OR If you appliqué (see pages 124-125): 2 pieces 20″ x WOF, then sew ends to together to make 1 piece 20″ x 84″.
Light Ribbon Color (Green)	⅜ yd (must be WOF)	All light ribbon templates For Piecing: Place template face down on back of fabric, trace around it, copy alignment marks in seam allowance, cut ¼″ outside of traced line. OR If you appliqué: Follow cutting instructions on page 110 for the appliqué method you are using.
Dark Ribbon Color (Dark blue)	¼ yd (can be FQ or WOF)	All dark ribbon templates. For Piecing: Place template face down on back of fabric, trace around it, copy alignment marks in seam allowance, cut ¼″ outside of traced line. OR If you appliqué: Follow cutting instructions on page 110 for the appliqué method you are using.
Backing and facing	2 yds	2 pieces 20″ x WOF, then sew ends to together to make 1 piece 20″ x 84″ for backing 4 strips 3″ x WOF. Sew ends together to make 2 strips 84″ long 1 strip 12″ x WOF, then cut in half to make two pieces 12″ x 21″
Batting	20″ x 84″	Choose a flat, dense batting such as Hobbs 80/20, not a puffy polyester or wool.
Fusible web (If you are using raw-edge appliqué) (Light-weight, MUST be paperbacked)	1 yd (15″ wide)	Fuse to back of light and dark ribbon template fabrics, then cut ribbon pieces from fused fabric.
Thread		For assembly: Match background fabric For satin stitch on edges of ribbon (If you are using raw-edge appliqué construction method): Coordinating color silk or shiny polyester For quilting: Match background fabric
Optional: Fabric glue		If using raw-edge appliqué, can be used for positioning ribbon sections instead of fusible web
Removable fabric marker, Permanent double-sided tape (for sticking templates to fabric)		

INSTRUCTIONS

NOTE: These instructions are for piecing. If you appliqué, follow the cutting instructions on page 110 and the assembly order on pages 124-125.

Build the Ribbon

1. Download and assemble the template from the Sideways Spirals Blog (see page 3 for address and password). Or, enlarge the template on the facing page using the method on page 138 in the *Flying Free* project. For the size shown here, squares in the full-size grid should be 4″ x 4″.

Make a second copy of Rows 1-3. Assemble and trim on the round line.

2. Cut the template into ribbon and background sections. Leave ends of runner square for now.

3. Using double-sided tape, place templates face down on the backs of their respective fabrics and trace around them to mark seam lines. Transfer all alignment marks. Cut out all pieces, adding approx. ¼″ seam allowance (see page 110).

4. Sew together in this order, using techniques on page 111.

> A1 to A2, add A3, then add A4 (4A).
> Repeat for section E.
>
> B1 to B2 to B3 and B4 to B5 (4B).
>
> Join the two B units, then add B6 (4C).
> Repeat for sections C and D (there is no D6).

5. Join Sections A, B, C, D and E (5).

6. Sew Backgrounds F and G to their respective sides (they are different). Sew Background H to "A" end and Background I to "E" end of ribbon.

Quilting

1. Layer top, batting and backing.

2. Stitch-in-the-ditch around the ribbon, inside and out.

3. Beginning at one end of the ribbon, shadow-stitch around it until the quilting reaches the outside edge. Use the edge of the foot as a guide.

4. Shadow stitch inside the squares and end loops.

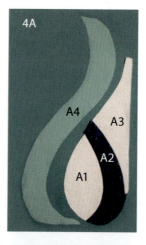

Facing

1. Trim sides straight and cut the ends round using the template made from the extra copy of Rows 1-3.

2. Press under ½″ along one edge of facing strips.

3. Place a 12″ x 21″ facing end piece face up on the table. Place the curved end of the runner face down over it. Pin, then trim facing fabric around the runner.

4. Turn runner face up. Pin facing strips face down along sides of runner. Where ends meet the round end facing piece, fold back both edges, line them up and pin.

5. Stitch the facing around the runner, ¼″ from raw edge.

6. Cut away the center of the end facing to a width of about 2½ inches. Hand stitch where folded edges of straight and curved facings join.

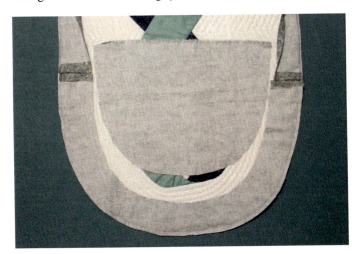

7. Notch seam allowance every ½″ around curve. Turn facing to back. Press well. Turn under raw edge of facing and blindstitch into place.

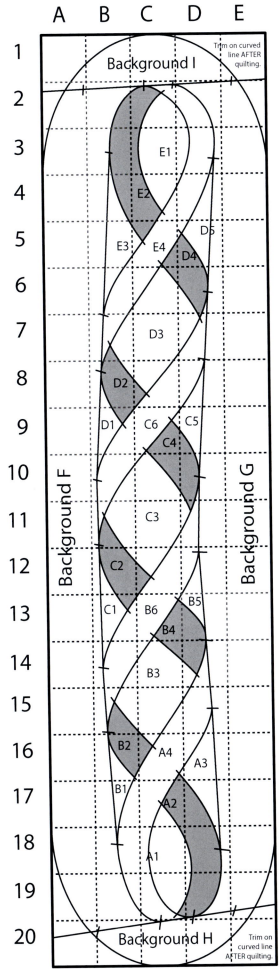

Resources

MY WEBSITE, ONLINE STORE & BLOG

Visit my website for information on workshops
www.ranaemerrillquilts.com

My main blog, for current news:
www.ranaemerrillquilts.wordpress.com

THE SIDEWAYS SPIRALS BLOG

www.sidewaysspirals.wordpress.com
Password: Si2de0waLys6

THREAD

Superior Threads
www.superiorthreads.com
Charlotte's Fusible Web Fusible Thread
Vanish Water-Soluble Thread
 Vanish-Lite for home machines
 Vanish-Extra for longarm machines
MonoPoly Invisible Polyester Thread
 Clear for light-colored fabrics
 Smoke for dark fabrics

BIAS TAPE MAKERS

Clover makes models both with and without the
channel for fusible tape. The model for fusible tape
can be used without it. Fusible tape is usually available where fusible tape models are sold. Several other
manufacturers make models for fabric only. Different
sizes are color-coded. Purchase at your local fabric
store or through my online store.

FUSIBLE WEB

There are a variety of products available, including:

Wonder Under by Pellon. Available at most fabric
shops. Use the regular weight 805, not the heavy 725.

Steam-a-Seam, The Warm Company
www.warmcompany.com

ALPHABET CHARMS

On the Sideways Spirals Blog
https://sidewaysspirals.wordpress.com/
alphabets-for-charms

PRINTABLE FABRIC SHEETS

EQ Printables Inkjet Fabric Sheets
Electric Quilt www.electricquilt.com
Available in a variety of weights and finishes.

RULERS & DRAFTING TOOLS

www.alvindrafting.com
The items shown on page 18 are:
Alvin Truflex II 24″ flexible ruler (Item #A1044-24)
French Curve template (Item #FC3371-01)
Many other styles are available.

STENCILING SUPPLIES

Cedar Canyon Textiles carries a wide variety of tools
for stenciling and fabric art, and has video tutorials
on how to use them. http://cedarcanyontextiles.com

This is a detail from the back
of Betsy Vinegrad's quilt *Spare
Change* (shown on page 1). The
name comes from the fact that,
after using a variation on the
Chinese Coins design for the
front, she used all the leftover
pieces to make the back. You
can see the complete back on
the *Sideways Spirals Blog.*

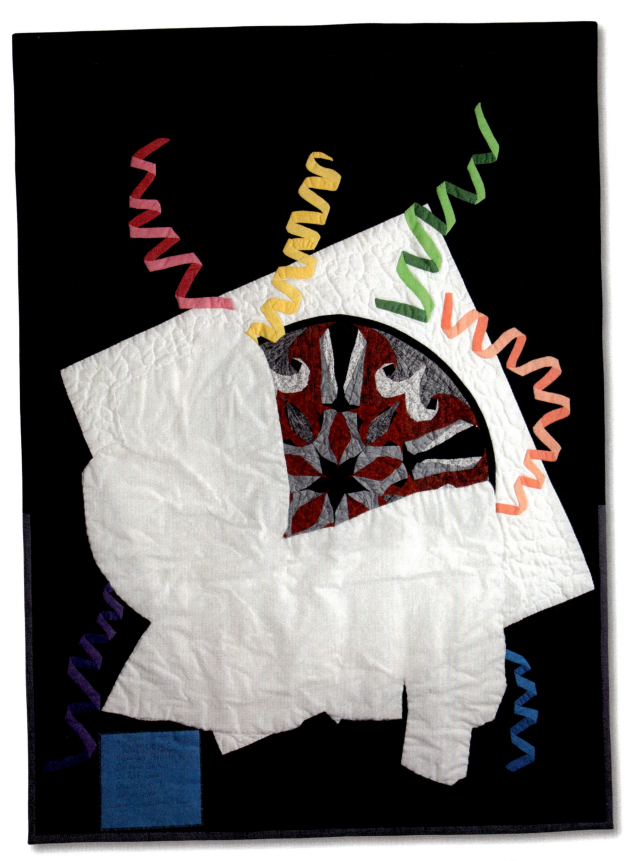

This is the back of Barbara Shirley's quilt *Surprise!* (shown on page 54). The "gift" is a spiral mandala based on my second book, *Magnificent Spiral Mandala Quilts*. Two spectacular quilts in one!

Index

More spiral quilts from RaNae Merrill

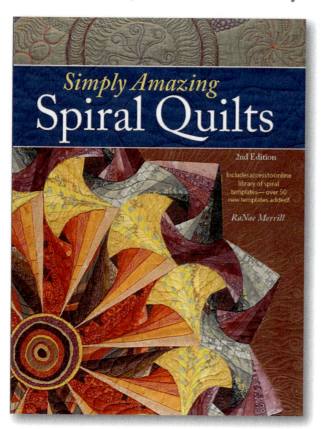

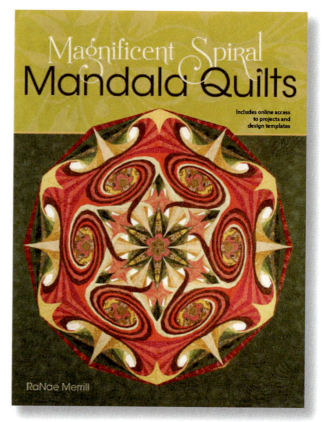

SIMPLY AMAZING SPIRAL QUILTS, 2ND EDITION

This is RaNae's best-selling first book on spiral quilt design. In this introduction to spirals, learn four types of spirals and variations on them, then explore a wide variety of spiral quilt settings. In this new edition, updated sewing techniques are easier than ever. Five projects are included, and the online library includes project templates, as well as hundreds of spiral blocks in a variety of shapes and sizes for you to use as the basis for your own unique spiral quilt designs.

Paperback, 8½˝ x 11˝
ISBN: 978-1-942853-00-8
www.createspace.com/5293179

MAGNIFICENT SPIRAL MANDALA QUILTS, 2ND EDITION

Don't let the extravagant quilt on the cover scare you—spiral mandala quilts are built on a simple variation of the Twisted Log Cabin block. You'll be surprised at how easy they are to design using mirrors and dry-erase markers. This new updated edition includes expanded design instructions and simplified sewing techniques. Even if you don't sew a spiral mandala, the photographs of over 50 exquisite mandala quilts make this volume a must-have just for the eye candy!

Paperback, 8½˝ x 11˝
ISBN: 978-1-942853-01-5
www.createspace.com/5407098

Made in the USA
Middletown, DE
29 March 2019